**Teacher-to-Teacher Series**

school-based CHANGE

D1313701

An NEA Professional Library Publication

Printing History
First Printing: March 1994

NOTE: The opinions expressed in this book should not be construed as representing the policy or position of the National Education Association. Materials published by the NEA Professional Library are intended to be discussion documents for educators who are concerned with specialized interests of the profession.

CREDITS: *Editor:* Mary Dalheim. *Production Coordinator:* Linda Brunson. *Art Design:* NoBul Graphics. Special thanks to Todd Endo of NEA Professional Standards and Practice for his editorial guidance.

Library of Congress Cataloging-in-Publication Data
School-based Change.
     p. cm. — (Teacher to teacher series)
    Includes bibliographical references.
    ISBN 0-8106-2905-4
    1. School-based management — United States. 2. Educational change — United States.
 I. NEA Professional Library (Association) II Series.
LB2806.35.S36 1994
371.2"00973—dc20   [20] 93-40578
               CIP

Contents

How to Use this Book

School-Based Change is no ordinary book. It is part of the NEA Professional Library's Teacher-to-Teacher book series in which classroom teachers speak directly to other teachers—like you— about their school restructuring efforts.

Printed in the upper right-hand corner of every book cover in the series is a routing slip that encourages you to pass the book on to colleagues once you have read it—in other words, to spread the word about school change.

Book topics cover areas such as large-scale school change, student assessment, cross-age grouping, and integrating students with special needs into regular classrooms.

Read the Six Stories

Inside each book you will find stories from six or more teachers across the country who discuss, step by step, how they tackled a specific restructuring challenge. They will describe what worked and didn't work, and provide you with any diagrams, checklists, or tables they think other teachers would find useful.

Write Your Own Ideas in this Book

At the end of each story in a book is an area called Reader Reflections. This area is for you and any colleague who reads the story to write related insights and action points for your school or school district to consider.

You see, the purpose of Teacher-to-Teacher books is not only to spread the word about school change, but to encourage other teachers to participate in its exploration.

Discuss Your Thoughts With Others

Once you have routed a Teacher-to-Teacher book through your school, you can meet with your colleagues who contributed to the Reader Reflections sections and expand upon your thoughts and suggestions.

Go Online

Believe it or not, the communication and sharing doesn't have to stop there. If you would like to discuss a Teacher-to-Teacher book topic with teachers across the country, you can. Any NEA member who subscribes to the America Online electronic network can participate in an ongoing forum on Teacher-to-Teacher book topics.

The National Education Association's area on the network is called NEA Online. Once signed on to NEA Online, just keyword to "NEA Prof/Library."

To subscribe to the NEA Online service, call 1-800-827-6364, ext. 8544.

Introduction

"You must not expect to be told what to do. You may not always know what to do next."

So read the principal's memo inviting teachers at Centreville Elementary in Fairfax County, Virginia, to join him, one local school administrator, and a handful of "change mentors" (education researchers) in initiating collaborative, school-based decision making.

That forewarning was addressed to the teachers in the first story of this book, but it easily could have been sent to teachers in any of the other five stories in *School-Based Change*. When each group of teachers rejected the old top-down paradigm for making decisions about school improvement, and accepted responsibility themselves for determining and meeting the needs of their schools, they became the navigators of relatively uncharted waters.

In each case, the journey encountered its share of obstacles. For example:

• At Centreville Elementary, initial meetings rambled on and on. These long discussions and ensuing digressions frustrated early attempts to set goals and "get to work" on what needed to be done.

• At Ahuimanu Elementary, in Kaneohe, Hawaii, teachers found there was never enough time to accomplish everything they had determined to do.

• At Diamond Middle School in Lexington, Massachusetts, teachers were forced several times to adjust their own carefully determined course for school change to meet new state and local reform mandates.

• At Jackson Road Elementary, some faculty members weren't sure they wanted to "buy into" a new system in which student teachers took over their classes while they worked on curriculum planning and teacher collaboration.

• In Gananda Community School District in Macedon, New York, two determined teachers fought a few rounds of the "but we've always done it this way" mentality before they were able to interest colleagues in experimenting with Outcome-Based Education in their K-5 school.

• And at Seneca Falls Middle School in Seneca Falls, New York, teachers were publicly ambushed by an ad hoc group of parents who opposed one of their change initiatives.

In all cases, these groups of teachers experienced more than a few moments of frustration, doubt, and even despair, but they quickly learned from these challenges, and the collegiality they developed among themselves led to a team spirit that could not be stopped. Looking back today, all of these groups can point with pride to tangible results in the area of school improvement, and just as important, they can point to exciting new goals and aspirations for the future.

What these teachers have learned is what most educators involved in school-based change discover at some point along the way — that school change is a complex, time-consuming, frustrating, continuing— but, yes — rewarding process.

If you are involved in school-based change, you will find the stories in this book extremely helpful. You will not only identify with the many trials and tribulations of these teachers, but will begin to detect some overall patterns in the process of initiating school change and be able to determine a set of change strategies that should work well in your school.

In other words, you will find that you are not alone, that many of the rough waters you encounter are a normal part of the change journey, that there are effective ways to navigate those waters, and that the results of the trip are well worth the effort.

—Mary Dalheim
Series Editor

Eleven Maxims of The Change Process

In *Teachers as Agents of Change (1992)*, Allan A. Glatthorn uses the research of Fullan (1990) and Louis and Miles (1990) to compile the following list of fundamental principles regarding school-based change.

You'll find that the six stories in *School-Based Change* reinforce much of this wisdom.

1. Large-scale participation at the initiation stage may be counter-productive.

2. The size of the change matters. The change should be large enough to require sustained efforts, but not so massive that it overwhelms participants.

3. Leaders should be flexible and multiple in their approach to change, blending top-down and bottom-up processes.

4. For change to be successful, administrators need both to apply pressure and provide support.

5. Changes in attitude often follow changes in behavior. Most people do not discover new meanings until they have tried something new.

6. Leadership that is strongly committed to a particular type of change is negatively related to the ability to adopt it. In other words, the leader who is positive that he or she knows exactly how things should be changed ignores the perceptions and ideas of others and thus runs the risk of failure.

7. While planning is important, complicated implementation plans can become a burden and a source of confusion.

8. Some problems are unsolvable. They are better left alone.

9. It is best to use "positive politics"— to focus on a few important priorities by implementing them well, while keeping other priorities in perspective.

10. Sometimes it is better to act and then plan. Effective action often stimulates interest in planning.

11. The most important priorities should be developing people and changing the culture of the organization. Placing those goals first develops the school's capacity for making effective change.

Notes:

_____

_____

_____

_____

_____

LEARNING A NEW DANCE

Collaborative, school-based decision making was a new and different concept for our faculty. Here is how we mastered the steps.

1

Invitation to The Dance

The Effective Schools Project at Centreville Elementary School in Fairfax County, Virginia, was born several years ago when our innovative, new principal decided to add risk taking to his repertoire of management skills. Quite unexpectedly, he announced that he had applied to the Fairfax County Public School (FCPS) Office of Research and Evaluation (ORE) to include our school in a special Effective Schools Project that would seek to initiate collaborative, school-based decision making — and furthermore — that Centreville had been accepted! At the time, this was a new and different concept for the entire faculty. His memo to teachers asked for personally devised applications from anyone interested in an opportunity for teacher leadership in determining and addressing the needs of the school. The memo was our "invitation to the dance" and contained two highlighted items:

"You must not expect to be told what to do.

You may not always know what to do next."

Members of
THE EFFECTIVE SCHOOLS COMMITTEE
Centreville Elementary School

Fairfax County, Virginia

The memo also covered the basic tasks of project members, which included attending monthly meetings; taking out-of-school visits; being open to new ideas and responsibilities; taking initiative to implement those ideas; focusing on planning and assessing progress to help low-achieving and underachieving students; and finally, and perhaps most important, being an agent for change and creating a vision for Centreville Elementary. This "Effective Schools Project" was going to be quite an undertaking!

For many different reasons, a number of us applied. Sherry Pulsinelli liked the idea of creating a vision, of being open to new ideas, and of having the opportunity to network with others outside the school building. Joanne McClelland Porello wanted to participate because of the effect that the group could have on underachievers, about

We were primed and ready to begin a synchronized activity to improve our school. What ensued was hardly synchronized.

whom she feels strongly. Kathryn DeCola felt that, as a new faculty member, this would be an ideal opportunity to get to know other faculty members while at the same time "become a driving force in developing a plan to improve the academic progress of low-achieving and underachieving students." Bobbi Vest saw this as an opportunity to be part of the decision-making process, and Suzan Davis confessed that she liked the idea of being included on a leadership team, but was skeptical at the same time. Then, too, a new county teacher-performance evaluation program was not far from the minds of some. Being involved in an effective schools program, perhaps, would enhance each teacher's effectiveness in the eyes of the evaluators.

The applications we submitted were as clever and unique as we were — some were serious and listed specific reasons for wanting to be involved; some were amusing, playing anagram-style games with names or offering dubious recommendations. As a result, a ubiquitous group, humorously called "The Centreville Seven," which included the five previously mentioned teachers as well as Carolyn Soderberg and Gail Chisholm, was ready to get started and meet the challenges of *something,* although we weren't exactly sure what. The invitation to the dance was accepted. We knew with *whom* we were going, but that was about all we knew.

Learning the Dance Steps

Our Centreville Seven joined the principal, several mentors invited by him from ORE — whom we assumed knew the ropes and would lead us by them — and one liaison person from our local administrative office. We would try to be a leadership group — a steering committee. We were primed and ready to begin a synchronized activity to improve our school. What ensued was hardly synchronized.

Kathryn claims she'll never forget that first meeting of the newly christened Effective Schools Committee (ESC). She expected "a clear picture of where we were headed by the end of that meeting...something concrete to take back to the faculty." What she got was "a great deal of frustration and mush."

Joanne recalls that "those first meetings were so vague, and people rambled on. It seemed like there was no focus, no actual goal, and I was frustrated because I wasn't sure my time was being used wisely. There were long discussions and digressions...."

Bobbi remembers that ESC meetings "tended to begin at 2:00 p.m. and end around dinnertime." Suzan, too, felt that we were meeting for hours, yet nothing seemed to get accomplished.

These weren't the only meetings we had. We knew that for this project to be valid, we needed faculty commitment, and so the committee conducted occasional faculty discussions. These were intended to be brief, but they became lengthy as well, as we brainstormed goals, characteristics of low-achievers and under-achievers, and priorities. Our ESC role seemed to

become one of generating endless ideas and seeking and clarifying vast amounts of information. At both ESC and faculty meetings, creative ideas flowed, discussion was valuable and energizing, but where were we going?

As a group, we were very product-oriented, but no product seemed forthcoming. We looked to the principal for help, but he purposely held back. He told us he wanted the group to become responsible for decisions, not to look to him for the answers. Our mentors from ORE and the local administrative office offered support and guidance, but they never took the lead on the dance floor. This was frustrating to us because we felt the ORE staff already knew the dance steps (because of their experiences with

other schools) and *should be* taking the lead; they seemed to be telling us we had to master the steps for ourselves. Sometimes it seemed as if they were waltzing while we tangoed (or tangled), and that the committee members themselves were listening to different rhythms. We thought we'd never master the steps. Of those times, Kathryn recalls, "a great deal of discussion — some heated, some on target, some misunderstood — but discussion nonetheless."

In retrospect, we feel that this frustration was an integral part of the change process. And the fact was that because more people were feeling ownership and there was greater schoolwide communication, we *were* making progress. We began to realize this, and hence, gained confidence and

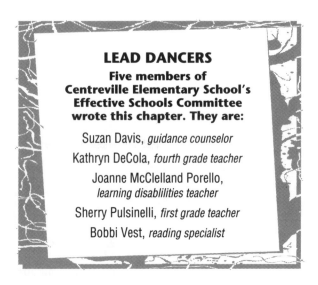

LEAD DANCERS

Five members of Centreville Elementary School's Effective Schools Committee wrote this chapter. They are:

Suzan Davis, *guidance counselor*

Kathryn DeCola, *fourth grade teacher*

Joanne McClelland Porello, *learning disabilities teacher*

Sherry Pulsinelli, *first grade teacher*

Bobbi Vest, *reading specialist*

saw potential for change even though the entire process still seemed very slow.

Choreographing The Dance

Midway through the first year, ORE sponsored a workshop day for the steering committees from several schools. Now, maybe we would get the answer we had been seeking: Just what should we be doing? The morning was very direct. First came small group discussion sessions with our counterparts from other schools.

They seemed to be dealing with different types of issues, from personnel problems to where to put coat closets. One faculty was learning to resolve conflicts. We realized that at Centreville we had some conflict, some disagreement, yet we were

Creative ideas flowed, discussion was valuable and energizing, but where were we going?

lucky because our differences were discussed, shared, and respected among members of the group. We were each able to appreciate the talents and thoughts of others and to see the whole picture from different perspectives. Some other

schools were obviously not so fortunate.

We also learned that some school-based administrators were reluctant to *really* share the decision making. We felt that one major factor in our success as a committee was having a principal who was willing to let loose "the reins of power." We were fortunate to have a principal who was also an integral part of the committee and who acted upon group decisions.

The second part of that workshop day dealt with the change process. The most important idea we took from this session was that *change* is a *process,* not an *event,* and can take as many as three to five years. We also learned these things about the process:

Change is complex, and sorting through choices for

change takes time.

Change is frustrating and ambiguous.

Change is a highly personal experience.

That workshop was valuable because we began to realize that the feelings we were having were quite natural in a change situation. Our feelings of frustration at our seeming lack of productive outcomes occurred because we were being asked to assume a new role. That role required new skills and information and using what we already knew in different ways. We all felt better to know others had the same feelings.

After lunch that day, we began to develop ideas for our own school plan to improve student achievement. We formulated objectives based on ideas collected previously from the faculty. At the work-

shop, we also heard for the first time that project funds might be available through a grant. We left the meeting with something concrete to work toward.

Although the prospect of getting needed money seemed exciting, the grant process became extremely frustrating. We invited anyone on the faculty interested in sharing ideas to come to a one-hour brainstorming session. The goal was to develop a list of ways to increase student achievement, given unlimited time and money. That one-hour meeting turned into four hours. Joanne aptly describes the day: "It made me frustrated, tense, and angry. There seemed to be no way to focus the group... another wasted day." Although emotions ran high, we did generate an exhaustive list of ways to improve student achievement.

From the ideas generated at the meeting, we later drafted an action-oriented product — a minority achievement grant proposal. This provided a plan for the dance. The ideas were outstanding, and we felt we really could *do something* that would make a difference for the children instead of just having meetings and talking on and on. Proudly, we sent the proposal off with high hopes. We had something tangible, and we believed in it.

Later that spring, our committee spent a day visiting a school that had been using a collaborative decision-making model for several years. We met with the school's steering committee and gained insight into the problems and successes the faculty had encountered.

At about this time, we realized that we, too, were a collaborative decision-making team. Consequently, the principal made us responsible for writing an official school planning document known as the Annual Operating Plan (AOP), the product of a planning process that is both facilitated and exacerbated by a framework of school board and county mandates.

First, we went to the faculty for its input. Then with funds from ORE , we arranged to have seven substitutes take our classes for a day, giving us an unencumbered eight-hour time block for drafting the planning document.

Just prior to that day, we found the grant proposal, of which we had been so proud, back on our doorstep, rejected by the Minority Achievement Grant Committee. Kathryn recalls her feelings: "I felt betrayed and angry. All that time and energy spent for nothing!"

Upon reflection, however, we recognized that conceptualizing, developing, and writing the grant proposal had solidified a feeling of ownership for our school committee. Each member had put a part of herself or himself into the proposal, and it could now form a basis for our AOP.

Much discussion, compromise, and revision eventually produced a school plan that represented the faculty's ideas and priorities. Our focus on low-achieving and underachieving students resulted in provisions for a late bus, home visits, and staff-development activi-ties. At the final faculty meeting in June, we presented and shared with pride and anticipation that plan as well as an organizational scheme for implementing its specific goals.

The organizational scheme included a steering committee (the original Centreville Seven) and subcommittees that focused on language arts, mathematics, and school

> *The communication that occurred at subcommittee meetings helped develop a team spirit.*

culture. Each faculty member was expected to join one subcommittee. Because there were three or four teachers for every

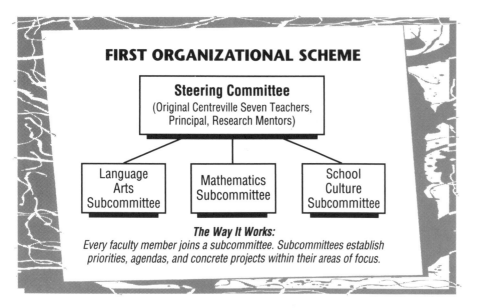

FIRST ORGANIZATIONAL SCHEME

Steering Committee
(Original Centreville Seven Teachers,
Principal, Research Mentors)

Language Arts Subcommittee

Mathematics Subcommittee

School Culture Subcommittee

The Way It Works:
Every faculty member joins a subcommittee. Subcommittees establish
priorities, agendas, and concrete projects within their areas of focus.

grade level, membership could be arranged so that every grade-level team had at least one representative on each subcommittee.

Now we needed a source of financial support to accomplish our goals. That support came from our superintendent, who recognized the merits of our proposal and funded a portion of the "ungranted" grant monies.

As our first school year closed, committee members' feelings of anger at the rejection of the grant proposal were softened greatly with the successful completion of the school planning document. But we were ready for a break from the dance — summer vacation!

Real Dancing

The new school year found us beginning work on our AOP goals in earnest. Because the new organizational format involved all of the faculty through committee membership, participation and collaboration among our teachers increased.

On the third Monday afternoon of school, the full faculty met. After brief, introductory remarks, individuals divided into their new subcommittees, elected a chairperson, chose a recorder, and determined their next meeting time. What a difference from the lengthy, unfocused meetings of the first year! Although our earlier stumbling had been a necessary part of the change process, this felt like the beginning of accomplishment.

Each of the three subcommittees surveyed all teachers and then established priorities, agendas, and concrete projects within their areas of focus. Thus a communication network developed that would link all the professionals in the building for information sharing and for collaborative planning. The process worked well. For example, the language arts subcommittee pulled from the school plan those objectives and work plans that pertained to language arts, then asked grade-level teams to submit their "wish lists" for implementation. Those requests were directed back through the subcommittee to the steering committee. The other subcommittees followed the same procedure. The beneficiaries were the students, as we ordered materials and developed programs to meet their needs. As Kathryn notes: "The communication that occurred at subcommittee meetings helped develop a team spirit.... We became aware of the needs of other grade levels and found many areas of commonality."

Not all went smoothly, however. Subcommittees realized that many of their objectives could not be accomplished without funds. They questioned whether the committees would have fiscal responsibility and be able to make decisions concerning spending.

The steering committee investigated what monies were available to the principal and how they were dispersed. For this year, we decided that teachers would request materials directly from the principal, and he would order them from available monies as he saw fit. While we recognized the principal's responsibility to oversee distribution of funds, the steering committee could and did coordinate fiscal allocations based on defined schoolwide needs. For example,

because we needed additional paperbacks to implement an integrated language arts program and because the Parent Teacher Association (PTA) particularly wished to support the reading program, faculty representatives obtained supplemental funding from the PTA. The language arts subcommittee dispersed the funds, based on grade-level team decisions; however, this was a cumbersome process for so small amount of money involved.

The focus of the steering committee soon turned to developing the final form of a data collection document. In light of recent research, our school was moving away from sole reliance on grades and test scores, and toward teacher observation to record low-

achieving and under-achieving students' progress. Also, some information being tracked was behavioral and fell into the area of teacher observation. Here again, essential elements became time for steering committee discussions and for returning to the faculty, and the principal's willingness to share responsibility (even to develop the format of the document on the computer). Lengthy philosophical dialogue centered on instruction, assessment, and differing views of evaluation. Continual input from faculty through subcommittees and from our out-of-school mentors helped to refine the document. The process led to an excellent product that provides valuable information for teachers, is easy for them to use, and is readily as-

similated into a school-wide data collection. By mid-October the document was ready and became the instrument to collect data on targeted low-achievers and under-achievers three times during the year: November, February, and May.

This second year of the Effective Schools Project also saw changes in the steering committee. One participant elected to devote more time to other pursuits, and we welcomed two chairs of subcommittees as well as a new assistant principal. We chose a committee chairperson to organize an agenda for and lead each meeting. Minutes of all meetings were first copied for teachers, then later, because of the paper blizzard that soon resulted, posted for all to read.

There was a marathon

of meetings during the fall semester; however, they tended to be shorter (often before school), and we felt more productive. In support of the school plan, the subcommittees had various projects in place by

By January of the second year, the steering committee was able to see tangible results from our efforts.

mid-year. These included:
• Teachers With Integrated Language Arts Goodies (TWIG), a voluntary bi-weekly before-school sharing session for teachers only;
• a mentor program involving specialists and underachieving students;
• the first quarterly awards ceremony;

• inservice training sessions on process writing and home visits;
• the ordering of math manipulatives and classroom book sets;
• teachers observing other teachers' language arts lessons both in and out of the school;
• a weekly late bus providing time for academic and incentive programs for targeted students; and
• plans for a business partnership.

The Centreville faculty had accomplished a great deal indeed!

Dancing Centre Stage

By January of the second year, the steering committee was able to see tangible results from our efforts. Targeted students were receiving extra help and attention from all staff. Clearly visible were

quarterly awards ceremonies; Student-of-the-Month bumper stickers; mentors and mentees; classes involved in weekly math team problem-solving activities; after-school instructional support sessions; and various clubs and student groups to support instructional programs and to improve school pride and spirit. There were also active programs for the teachers to inspire and support their work. Most mornings before school we could find meetings (e.g., subcommittee, team, TWIG, and others) in the media center or in classrooms. Everyone on the steering committee was involved in committee work of every sort.

News of our project spread beyond our doors as others wanted to learn of our activities and were

excited about our results. Centreville Schools took "Centre Stage" — we became noticed not only throughout our local administrative area, but throughout the Fairfax County Public Schools system. Three steering committee members were invited to share our experiences with other schools just entering the Effective Schools Project. There was a pervasive "electricity" throughout the school as our Business Partnership Celebration Day neared, and excitement grew over an upcoming visit from the superintendent, school members, and other notables. The school's Teacher Resource Files filled with exciting ideas, and we awaited the arrival of books, software, and videos that would supplement the instructional programs. All classroom teachers were directly responsible for the evaluation and selection of newly adopted language arts materials and for establishing priorities for purchasing those materials. Class banners, designed and made by the students, proudly decorated the school; and students from the new welcoming, cleanup, and school beautification committees could be seen at work.

In the middle of January, our research office mentors, working from the data we had collected, returned the first report on the targeted underachieving students. The research staff had provided statistical sheets with columns of percentages for each evaluated area and had produced bar graphs to make the results more visually appealing

and easier to comprehend. We reviewed our data collection document to determine if we were getting the information that we really wanted, and if the form had been a successful tool for teachers to use. We concluded it had.

In February, when the teachers again completed the data collection document, we awaited the results to see if statistics would prove what we already sensed — that our Effective Schools Project was indeed effective. Because the staff and the principal collaborated, ideas were put into action and success could be measured in statistical improvement in tracked areas over the year. This collaboration strengthened a schoolwide perspective. Research office staff members continued quietly and unobtrusively

to hand the responsibilities over to us, heading us toward the self-sufficiency for which we were ready.

At the end of February, we spent a day sharing our ideas, experiences, and problems with other Effective Committees. We explored ways in which the decision-making process was evolving in the different schools, and what supported or inhibited the process. Our observations and those of teachers at other schools were amazingly similar, in spite of the fact that each program was tailored to individual school needs. We agreed that this project was benefiting communication within our schools, and that the many meetings required to implement the program enhanced human relations and teamwork. How-

ever, the snags were also similar — whole staff or large group meetings got out of hand and were lengthy, and teachers felt that they simply didn't have enough time to do what they were hired to do — TEACH.

That afternoon, during our individual school meetings, we reviewed the results of the February data collection and were thrilled with them: positive movement in all areas! As we examined our school plan, it became evident that we *were* meeting our school's goals for students. We debated how to present the results to the already overburdened faculty, and how to ask members for more feedback on the data collection process we had developed. Then Sherry suggested that we present the information to the faculty as a celebration. "Take a Bite out of the AOP" became the theme, complete with decorated cake and party favors. The approach was very effective.

By March, TWIG meetings had become extremely popular. There was an abundance of presenters as well as participants. Teachers loved sharing ideas and learning from

It takes a lot of time to be involved in shared decision making, but the effort has been worth it because our children have benefited.

each other. The math subcommittee continued its work on the weekly math questions and shared new software. The large number of members and the extensive responsibilities of the school culture subcommittee had created logistical problems, so the faculty decided that redefining roles for the next year would be necessary.

April came, and with it, more demands on teachers' time. Handicapped Awareness Week, Career Awareness Week, and preparation for authors and artists displays in May, took up what little extra time anyone had. Meetings continued, TWIG maintained its popularity, and textbooks and materials were selected. At the area superintendent's request, a group from the steering committee presented our project to the principals of the area's 35 elementary schools. As a result, there were numerous requests for more information. The data collection process was viewed as a useful tool.

By the end of May, at our second planning day, we all felt that we really had accomplished something special, powerful, and meaningful. The third set of statistics had been collected and tallied, and further improvement in the data was evident. When each subcommittee's final report was reviewed, we were pleased with our results.

We focused on needs and modification necessary for continued progress, then developed the Annual Operating Plan for the coming year. Three factors would mandate change: a drastically reduced student population due to redistricting, a resultant loss of several teachers, and questions about subcommittee roles. The Effective Schools Project at Centreville would continue to evolve.

Reflections: The Dance Continues

Today we can see that much good has been accomplished through the work of this committee and of the entire faculty. The steering committee believes we were successful because teachers saw that their opinions mattered: their recorded observations for student progress were acted upon and their ideas for specific activities were implemented. We asked faculty members for help and showed them what we did with their suggestions. We celebrated our successes, and everyone felt they had a part in the changes made.

It takes a lot of time to be involved in shared decision making, but the effort has been worth it because the children in our classes have benefited. We recognize that we can't change a child's ability, but as our data show, we can change his or her success in school!

Would these changes have occurred at our school anyway? Would the activities have developed? Would we have had a late bus or $1,600 from the PTA, or banners, or award ceremonies, or math teams? We don't know for sure. Some of this might have happened anyway. Would the school's common sense of purpose and spirit or camaraderie have been the same? We don't think so. Was it worth the time and energy? YES!

Our project continues, getting stronger each year because we have sound, positive, collaborative leadership. We have welcomed support from ORE and our local administrative area. They help us go in the right direction and execute the dance steps. And finally, we have interested and concerned staff members who want to move our school and its students further toward excellence. Our changes in attitude and process were not easy, but they were important because we created them together. We like that. ◆

TURNING POINTS ◆ Learning a new dance was an evolving process for Centreville Elementary School. The following are points in the process where significant change occurred.

Year 1, Day 1

◆ Centreville joins the Effective Schools Project (ESP) of Fairfax County Public Schools in Virginia. The project's goal is to use collaborative decision making to develop ways to improve student achievement, particularly in low-achieving and under-achieving students.

Year 1, Semester 1

◆ Seven teachers, one principal, and a handful of research mentors form the Effective Schools Committee (ESC). Initial meetings of ESC generate many ideas, but no real plans for action.
◆ ESC meets with entire faculty. More ideas; still no hard-core product. High level of frustration.

Year 1, Semester 2

◆ ESC hears about available grant monies. With full faculty input, it drafts a minority achievement proposal that includes plans for staff development training, after-school instructional support for students, and additional curriculum materials.
◆ The proposal is rejected.
◆ ESC and faculty decide to incorporate these ideas and others into the school's Annual Operating Plan (AOP).
◆ Superintendent recognizes the merits of the proposal and provides additional funding.

Year 2, Semester 1

◆ Entire faculty divides into three subcommittees to accomplish the AOP plans and to generate still others.
◆ Plans are set in motion for many activities.

Year 2, Semester 2

◆ These activities are implemented: quarterly award ceremonies, mentorships, a business partnership, classes in weekly math problem-solving activities, instructional support sessions for students, various clubs and student groups to improve school pride and spirit.
◆ Statistical improvement in student achievement occurs in tracked areas over the year.

Insights: _____

_____

_____

_____

_____

_____

Actions for Our School (District) to Consider: _____

_____

_____

_____

_____

_____

_____

_____

_____

MATTERS OF TIME

The school change process involves important matters of time. Attending to those matters is crucial to affecting change.

2

I ducked as another unfamiliar term was thrown my way at the first faculty meeting I had attended in four years. I hadn't anticipated that so many changes would occur during the time I had taken off to raise my baby. Integration...computer networking...teacher empowerment...authentic assessment...mastery in learning...were some of the new issues being discussed. A teacher stood in the front of the room, leading the faculty to relook at a school vision that included parent and community involvement.

Well, I thought as I looked at the sign-up lists for the year's committees, I might as well go for it and find out what this is all about. I signed up for the restructuring committee. Little did I know I was about to embark on a challenging, but rewarding, adventure.

It took me more than a

MARGARET ALMONY
Special Education Teacher
Ahuimanu Elementary School
Kaneohe, Hawaii

year to start to understand the process of change that was occurring at Ahuimanu Elementary School in Kaneohe, Hawaii. The school had been part of an NEA-sponsored Mastery-in-Learning Project through which it had developed a teacher-driven school improvement process. As part of the process, the faculty identified school and student needs and formed committees to work on improving these areas in our school. The committees then discussed possible solutions, explored research, dialogued with other Mastery-in-Learning schools, and proposed changes to the administration and faculty.

Due to my membership in the restructuring committee, I was able to attend workshops on effective schools as well as a national Mastery-in-Learning conference. I became excited about the possibilities that were presented to improve education for our students and to empower teachers to be a part of the restructuring process. I discussed the teacher empowerment opportunities with our principal, Mrs. Inada, and as a result, she encouraged me to develop a proposal to implement site-based management at Ahuimanu School.

This is where my story really begins because this

We became a "council of leaders," with a shared vision of improving our school.

is where I first came to realize that the school change process involves important matters of time and that mastering these is crucial to affecting change.

Time to Communicate

Initially, I thought that because of Ahuimanu's involvement in Mastery in Learning, which included a focus on change to improve the school, the faculty would welcome my site-based management proposal. I had not anticipated that teachers would interpret it as yet another layer of work with even more committee meetings!

I scrambled to provide more information to teachers about Hawaii's experimental site-based management system, talked individually with teachers, and searched for research on site-based management in other schools that would support my case. I was lucky to have access to an NEA/IBM-sponsored computer network called the School Renewal Network.

Online, I tapped into researcher Doug Fleming's helpful information on managing change and restructuring. I also communicated with teachers in others parts of the country. The teachers on the network served as a sounding board for each other; we all struggled to identify and solve problems.

After more meetings and further discussion, the faculty did agree to become a site-based school.

Then came the task of meeting with other members of our school community to secure their agreement and involvement in developing a proposal to become a site-based school. Suddenly, time became a critical issue in my life. I found that not only was I trying to juggle a teaching career, but I was in constant discourse with parents, stu-

dents, staff, administration, and teachers from the time I left my car in the morning to late in the afternoon. While I thought the process was important, I began to wonder if I was too idealistic in thinking that site-based management would be "manageable."

I started to dialogue with other schools on the School Renewal Network to see if they had found any answers to this time dilemma. Again, I found support and ideas from other schools, and it became even more apparent to me that communicating was a vital part of school restructuring. I came to realize that by sharing our ideas, successes, and failures, we can eliminate the need to "reinvent the wheel" and indeed save ourselves some time while helping others.

Time to Delegate

My responsibilities grew when I was elected chairperson of Ahuimanu's first SBMC (site-based management council). To my husband's chagrin, our house was soon piled with papers, articles, and file folders. While I enjoyed the challenge, I began to wonder if meeting my new professional responsibilities would be possible. I still needed to create lesson plans, teach, and serve on school committees.

As I mumbled a discouraged, "Whew, am I going to be able to do all this?" I suddenly heard a, "How can we help?" from my co-workers, Doreen Yamashiro and Grace Ing. I looked up in great relief and realized I had forgotten one of the cardinal rules of leadership — delegate.

Others soon pitched in, too. Our student representatives on the council were eager to lead team-building activities. A parent arranged for a speaker to come to a meeting to discuss the "school within a school" concept. And our vice principal would leave pertinent articles in my mailbox that addressed various issues we were discussing.

I suddenly knew what true "site-based management" meant; and we became a "council of leaders" with a shared vision of improving our school. By dividing responsibilities, the time each person spent became more manageable.

Meanwhile, membership in the restructuring committee more than doubled to a respectable size of 11. Wow! How wonderful to see faces of other excited teachers who had become interested in restructuring by attending conferences, reading articles, and joining the School Renewal Network. Together, we looked at what was happening at Ahuimanu and tried to make sense of the layers of committee structures, pilot projects, projected changes, and current directives from the state that we were trying to implement.

Time to Consolidate

Soon our school became a smorgasbord of changes. We had been enticed to try a little of this and a little of that. But somehow, we didn't realize that by attempting to do so much, we were making slow progress in everything. I began to have long talks with one of the other teachers about our lack of a clear focus. It became evident that although our intentions were good, we had taken on too many major projects. Teachers were burning out and becoming disenchanted by the fact that we were meeting more often, but didn't seem to be accomplishing tangible improvement in any area. As the restructuring committee explored this issue, we discovered that while the school had added new projects, we had not discarded items from the past. We still retained the curricula committee structure and had added committees in global awareness, character development, and communication skills (not to mention the

THE SMORGASBORD OF CHANGE

Ah, the table is laden with dishes that delight the eyes and whet the appetite. We take a plate and slowly move down the line, scooping a taste of this and a smidgen of that, trying to keep room for all the items we see piled high — yet we still try to fit something new on without having it all run together.

Eagerly, we sit down with friends to sample our amazing feast. The variety and tastiness please us. Comments of delight and enjoyment encourage us to think about returning for second helpings so that we can taste those things that we didn't try the first time. But, then, what about the dessert table?

I sometimes wonder whether we as educators aren't also being "invited" to a smorgasbord. The "table" has a wide array of changes sitting on it, including co-operative learning, technology, site-based management, integrated curriculum, multi-age grouping, whole language, and the list continues. But, are our plates becoming too full? Are the changes piled so high that they run into each other and ruin the taste or palatability?

Granted, many changes seem to need to go hand in hand in order to succeed. But, I'm wondering if we aren't taking on a little too much. It's difficult to limit ourselves when there is such an emphasis on the need for change, and we are being criticized from all angles on our past educational practices. But managing so many changes is difficult. And evaluating our accomplishments becomes even harder.

professional development, technology, and restructuring committees). We had also continued to retain the old paradigm of a yearly curricula budget plan.

It was no wonder that teachers were dismayed by the amount of committee meetings they had to attend. Classroom planning time had become a thing of the past. The restructuring committee puzzled continuously over how to effectively consolidate curricula, the Mastery-in-Learning program, site-based management, and grade level and budget committees. We finally came up with a working model to present to the faculty.

Unfortunately, old patterns and paradigms die hard. Although we had tried to combine and integrate committees, there were some teachers who had a difficult time visualizing the change and needed a detailed explanation of how it was all "going to work." The administration was leery of giving up the curricula budget plan, anticipating that the school would not focus on necessary curricula purchases. We began to wonder if our plan was indeed workable.

Remeeting, the restructuring committee again charted committee responsibilities and possible regrouping. We revised things according to the feedback we had received from the faculty and in a way that would satisfy the administration's concern about program funding. Then we presented our revised proposal and after much discussion and adjustment, all agreed to try our new structure for a year, making ongoing changes as needed.

Time to Restructure Time

Time, however, continued to be mentioned as a major obstacle in affecting change and improvement. Teachers recognized the need for time to dialogue and research. A Mastery-in-Learning grant provided us with funding for substitutes to cover classrooms, but we were all wondering whether this was the best alternative. Maxine Haun, one of our teachers, commented that her students had complained, "We're going to have a substitute again?" Many of us had experienced similar comments. We also discussed the need for total faculty discourse and cross-level articulation. The restructuring committee agreed that we should focus on this aspect of time.

The teachers on the restructuring committee were determined to produce at least one workable solution to our time dilemma. We met one Friday afternoon and went on into the evening charting, scheduling, comparing, laughing, grumbling, and "maybe-ing." How could we do it? We discussed setting up a school week in which students

attended four longer days instead of the regular five (using Hawaii's Maile School as a model). But we wondered if we could really expect the students to be able to attend longer school days. We also were concerned that we did not have the vast funds that Maile had to implement this plan. Maxine Haun presented some of the ways schools on the School Renewal Network were trying to solve this problem. We also discussed having other professionals free up grade levels by teaching art, music, and P.E. But we realized that coming up with salaries for these professionals was a "dream on" situation.

We then became interested in the possibility of changing our weekly schedule a little through changes in recess time

and prep time to allow for one Friday off a month for teachers to meet at school. We would eliminate five minutes of recess a day and change one prep period a week to instructional time. This would make up for the instructional time students would miss on that one Friday a month. Encouraged by actually coming up with a proposal, we approached the principal to arrange for a faculty meeting to discuss our ideas.

Optimistically, we presented our proposal to reschedule time to our faculty. Oops! The questions, concerns, and resistance to it were staggering. Slowly, we answered, discussed, reworded, and brainstormed solutions to these concerns. The faculty then agreed to try the proposal.

Our restructuring committee, however, began to

have doubts. How were we going to manage child care for the students on that one free Friday a month? Who was going to administer the program? What would the parents' reactions be to our proposal? Back to the drawing board to look at possible alternatives. After puzzling again and again over time schedules, we were able to develop a

Somehow, we didn't realize that by attempting to do so much, we were making slow progress in everything.

more manageable alternative. This time, we rescheduled starting time and recess time to "create" an extra hour at the end of the day on Wednesdays to meet. The school's after-school program graciously agreed to work with us to provide child care during this extra hour.

Our new proposal was much more enthusiastically received and agreed to by the faculty. The parents also agreed to a year's trial of the proposal. We

Take time to rejoice in accomplishment and consensus.

quickly sent a request to the district to approve our idea. Anxiously, I looked for the superintendent's reply. It stated:

"We commend you for finding a workable solution to your school's time dilemma."

Now to work out the kinks and try to implement the program! We hope to start in 1994.

Time to Celebrate

What's next on the agenda? Celebration! School change takes an incredible amount of energy, time, and commitment. It is not an easy journey, and it is important to take the time to rejoice in accomplishment and consensus. This should also be a time to thank everyone for their hard work and to validate team cohesiveness. We believe that by celebrating, we can re-energize ourselves, renew feelings of self-worth, and rise to meet the challenges of continued school improvement.◆

Five Timely Words For Affecting Change

Communicate

Take the time to provide teachers with enough information and research so that they feel comfortable making and implementing decisions. Otherwise, anxiety and lack of support may set in and cause a need for even more time to be taken to smooth out and rework problems.

Also allow time for teachers to share and communicate with their peers. By supporting each other, teachers can relieve some of the stress associated with change and can share ideas to make the tasks less overwhelming.

Delegate

The concept of leadership has changed from principal-as-leader to shared leadership. By spreading leadership roles and responsibilities throughout the school community and rotating leadership, all teachers can grow and provide ongoing renewal to the change process. This eliminates some of the burnout that occurs when only a few people in the school are overloaded with a lack of time to do an effective job.

Delegate roles and responsibilities in committees. This decreases the amount of work for each person and increases the amount of ownership for projects by committee members.

Consolidate

Schools often add new projects or curricula to what already exists. At some point, we need to eliminate what is unnecessary and prioritize what remains.

As site-based management was introduced to our original school structure, we found ourselves faced with overlapping committees, too many committees, and an overwhelming list of "things to do." If possible, consolidate committees so that personnel is not so scattered and time is more manageable.

Restructure

There are numerous ways to "find" much-needed planning time. Look and see if schedules can be juggled; if teachers can be relieved by support staff, substitutes, or parents; or if classes can team up.

Celebrate

Take the time to celebrate! Change is not an easy journey. It takes time, energy, and commitment to affect change. By celebrating, we re-energize ourselves to take on new challenges and refine past practices.

Reader Reflections

Insights: _____

_____

_____

_____

_____

Actions for Our School (District) to Consider: _____

_____

_____

_____

_____

_____

_____

"Reform cannot be carried out during teachers' spare time. If reform is to be effective, the job description of the teacher has to change."

Gene Maeroff
The Empowerment of Teachers

SEASONS OF CHANGE

The way I see it, school change is a continuous cycle of four seasons.

3

It's October again. As I sit at my desk, looking at the majestic white pines outside my window, I know they are changing before my eyes. Last week all the needles were green. Today the trees look ill, with half their needles brown. By next week, I know there will be a pile of dead needles on the ground, and only a very few remaining green ones will be productive. But during the coming winter months, with very little showing on the outside, there will be an invisible reorganization taking place inside my trees, so that by next May, they will burst forth with a new crop of young green needles, growing on sunbathed branch tips. My trees will flourish anew through the summer months until October is once again here (even though the scars of past cycles will always remain along older stems and branches). I could easily miss one year's growth because the change is so small. Yet, 10 year's hence, when these trees shade out their neighbors, the accumulated small changes will be impossible to miss.

Why do I use this scene to open my story about school change? Because I am a biologist who teaches life science, and this is my metaphor for the process of school change.

LAURA P. KRICH

Seventh Grade Science Teacher
Diamond Middle School
Lexington, Massachusetts

The way I see it, school change is a continuous cycle of four seasons. The timing of these seasons may differ from Mother Nature's, but the basic characteristics are the same. We have to let go of the needles of our old ideas and practices in the fall (yet keep what works); permit time for new information and ideas to foment during our winter dormancy; and after a springtime of renewal, these new ideas (needles) will have a summer to grow and flourish. Then, as it must, the cycle will repeat.

From my personal experiences with school change, I think winter is the most difficult season to survive. It is the time when it is easiest to give up and allow new ideas to die because the impending changes are not yet visible. I have more patience for winter these

teaching biology in a high school in Lexington, Massachusetts, to teaching sixth grade general science in the town's new middle grade configuration, Diamond Middle School.

Changing schools and making the professional adjustment from dealing

part of a five-member team that was to lead Diamond's 450 or so students and 50 staff members into the Mastery-in-Learning Project, a teacher-driven school improvement process sponsored by the National Education Association (NEA).

tary schools, two middle schools that consist of grades six through eight, and one four-year high school. There are still active farms in town, along with new biotech and other high tech companies. The townspeople are proud of our schools, our community services, and our heritage.

A Setting with Still More Challenges

It would be helpful for you to know more about the setting of this story. Lexington (yes, the same town where the American Revolution began) is a suburban community about 15 miles west of Boston, with an area slightly over 25 square miles and a population between 25,000 and 30,000. With a school population between 4,000 and 5,000, we currently support five K-5 elemen-

In my mind, our will to persevere has come from working with a very committed principal and with the contacts we have made with other educators across the nation ...

days, though, because I know from experience that the resurgence of spring, though perhaps delayed, will indeed come.

The Cycle Begins

My story actually begins in September 1986, when I chose to move from

with the intellectual needs of advanced placement students to the more emotional needs of sixth graders seemed like a tall enough order. But change seems to find me, and I was further challenged by the school's principal, Eugene Sullivan, to become

Since 1973, when I became a Lexington teacher, I have steadily watched the school enrollments decrease by half. We are just now beginning the slow climb back. You can well imagine the impact. Our staffing has remained stable with most attrition resulting from retirements. New hires were a very small percentage of staff. I myself was told during 16 of my 18 teaching years that there might not be a job for me the next year.

The formerly generous funding for our school budget has become level funding. Our Proposition 2 1/2 has severely limited increases in the local property tax base, which is the major school funding source. For years now, more than 90 percent of the school system's operating budget has been designated for salaries, due to the seniority of our staff. Obviously, Lexington's ability to fund major innovations comes close to nil.

When Diamond Middle School began it's participation in the Mastery-in-Learning Project, not only were we beginning our work in a stagnant economic environment, but we were soon to be challenged by additional setbacks.

Three years ago all schools in our district were subjected to a con-tractually specified, mandated school improvement program, and last year the state of Massachusetts handed down its own mandated school-reform measures. With each new superimposed mandate, we have needed to change course from the successful paths we have established for ourselves and adapt to a new pre-scribed course.

If that is not enough, we lost a much loved principal to a year's very visible bout with cancer, the superintendancy has been held by five different persons in eight years, our associate superintendent for curriculum has changed three times during the same period, and we had to weather a week-long teachers' strike after four months of work-to-rule.

Nevertheless, against these great odds, we at Di-amond have set in motion highly successful proce-dures for improving the educational environment for all our schools' inhabi-tants. In my mind, our will to persevere has come from working with our current and very com-mitted principal, Joanne Hennessy, and with the contacts we have made with other educators across the nation who are also engaged in the process of improving schooling.

Year One

As I said earlier, our school change process can be traced back to 1986 when we joined the Mas-tery-in-Learning Project (MILP). Two basic premis-es of this school-change initiative are:

1. Systemic school change can begin with the teachers.

2. Teachers need quick, easy access to accurate research information in order to make informed decisions about change.

After visiting Diamond Middle School for the first time, MILP directors Bob McClure and Sylvia Sei-del, along with an assistant, Shari Castle, prepared a profile of our school for us. It included the following observations:

1. Lexington teachers place more emphasis on the knowledge base than do the administrators.

2. Teachers use lecture as the most frequent technique with some lab, inquiry, and cooperative learning.

3. Teachers see themselves as resource people, *not* as fellow learners.

4. When it comes to professional development, there is a large discrepancy between what Lexington teachers want and what they have. Teachers want more opportunity to seek constructive criticism from colleagues; they want to improve their classroom practice through classroom observation, and they want the time and opportunity to coordinate lesson plans and teaching strategies with colleagues.

During this visit, Bob, Sylvia, and Shari also asked us to describe our ideal school of the future. They listed these aspirations, or "imagings," for us as well. They included:

Students: To be confident, independent, and highly motivated; to enjoy school; to feel successful

Classes: To be small, relaxed, and flexible; to provide large-group, small-group, and individual instruction

Learning Activities: To be varied, interdisciplinary, hands-on, active, and meaningful; to involve problem solving; to meet individual needs

Materials: To be readily available, up-to-date, varied, and on-time; to include computers and audio visuals

Schedule: To be flexible

Administration: To be supportive

Communication: To be open and trusting between and among all combinations of teachers, students, parents, aides, and administrators

Teachers: To have planning time, to function as facilitators and resource managers, to have positive and helpful evaluation opportunities

Building: To have planning areas and clean and flexible space

Plus: To have no bells,

hall passes, or detention.

Our school steering committee reviewed the MILP data carefully, and after seemingly endless debate and discussion (as always) recommended four areas for priority action:

1. Grouping and Flexible Scheduling

2. Teachers Learning From One Another

3. Lack of Confidence in Teachers' Evaluation

4. Communication.

We brought the proposal to the faculty in February, and after more seemingly endless debate and discussion, faculty members reshaped the proposal into these five priority areas:

1. Advisor/Advisee Program

2. Grouping/Flexible Scheduling

3. Learning Styles

4. Critical Thinking/ Problem Solving

5. Team Structuring.

(*Note: We continue to set priorities such as these. See sidebar on current priorities, pp. 4.*)

At about the same time we were conducting these long and frustrating discussions, our steering committee chair, Amy Wagner, wrote and received funding for a local Horace Mann grant to permit reciprocal peer observation by teachers. Our newly hired site consultant, Jane Gaughan, arranged the training and pairings for these sessions. The funding let us hire substitutes to cover teachers during school hours and to pay a small stipend to participating teachers for after-school training sessions. The original group of five pairs of staff members was so enthusiastic that it asked the committee to repeat the project the following year.

And that's how year one ended: one very small project off the ground, yet increasing frustration over how long everything else was taking.

Year Two

Year two began with new frustrations. We returned to school in a work-to-rule situation because we had no contract. How could our committees work after school hours and volunteer to do things we wanted to do under these conditions?

Everything was on hold, or so it seemed. As I look back now, however, I see we weren't on hold at all. We were internally reorganizing our resources to meet these new conditions. We just didn't know it at the time. One event stands out in my mind. In October of 1987, teams from all the Mastery-in-Learning Schools met in Minneapolis at the Scanticon Conference Center. We were treated to talks by Ted Sizer of the Coalition of Essential Schools who urged us to "challenge the regularities"; by researcher Ann Lieberman, who in a small group presentation on change in schools, said what I remember as "critical mass for change in school can be a very small percentage of the faculty, in fact, it can be as small as one committed individual who won't give up"; and by education researcher Pat Wasley who listed six types of skills needed to foster a more professional culture: (1) trust and rapport building, (2) organizational analysis, (3) group process skills, (4) resource tap-

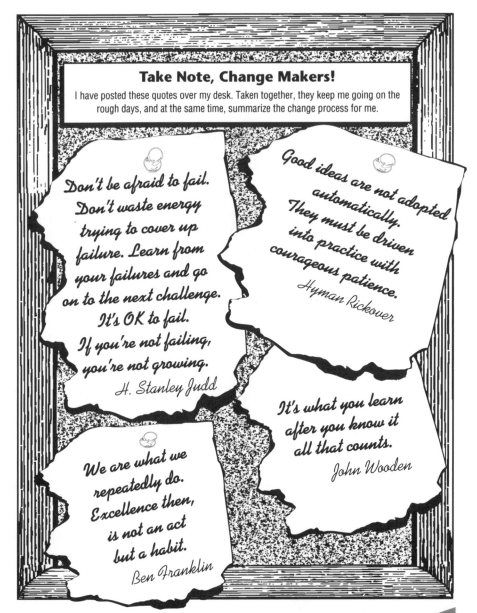

Take Note, Change Makers!

I have posted these quotes over my desk. Taken together, they keep me going on the rough days, and at the same time, summarize the change process for me.

Don't be afraid to fail. Don't waste energy trying to cover up failure. Learn from your failures and go on to the next challenge. It's OK to fail. If you're not failing, you're not growing.

H. Stanley Judd

Good ideas are not adopted automatically. They must be driven into practice with courageous patience.

Hyman Rickover

We are what we repeatedly do. Excellence then, is not an act but a habit.

Ben Franklin

It's what you learn after you know it all that counts.

John Wooden

ping, (5) work management, and (6) skill and confidence building in others.

These were very inspirational gatherings, but at the same time, in small discussions, in corridors, at meals, and while walking together, I sensed that although every school

cause on our third day together, as we spoke in groups, we began to realize our problems weren't related to the task of what we were trying to improve in our individual schools; our problems sounded more and more as if we were hitting a wall in the change process itself, and

know where it was taking us? I can't speak for others who were at Scanticon with me, but I have never forgotten that moment of truly internalizing this view of change as a process with a life of its own. I can still picture where I was standing in the hallway when this insight hit. I use this insight regularly even now as I ask myself if we are focusing on the process or the product.

The solution was to use one of our five curriculum release half-days for a study session for the entire staff. My committee also sensed a need to meet off-campus in a more comfortable environment. But where? I volunteered my home.

The steering committee elected to share information on cooperative learning and learning styles. We divided 45 staff members into eight groups. We gave each group eight different articles on cooperative learning. Each group member read one article and summarized it aloud for the rest of the group. No two people in any one group read the same article, but each group had the same collection from which to choose. Discussion was lively and continued into the building in the succeeding days.

Everything was on hold, or so it seemed. As I look back now, however, I see we weren't on hold at all. We were internally reorganizing our resources to meet these new conditions.

present had chosen different tasks to address in its first year, all of us had the same feelings of frustration. Some schools were ready to quit and drop out of the project. I wasn't alone in sensing this be-

we were all hitting it at the same time.

Did this process of change have a life of its own? Was there a course we were running without ever having had a chance to preview it? Did we

Sharing New Information

By this time I was the steering committee chair at Diamond and I wanted to *do* something with colleagues to share the new information we had received at Scanticon and from other sources. We were still under work-to-rule sanctions, so it had to be during regular hours.

Our copier was also busy as we filled out requests from staff for copies of the articles they had heard about, but had not personally read.

Exploring Group Process

Given the sense of stagnation the steering committee was feeling, (after all, we had done nothing yet on the five priorities we had painfully established the previous year), the Mastery-in-Learning Project directors sent educational consultant Karen Spencer to Lexington to meet with the steering committee for a day on the topic of group process.

Karen is knowledgeable, inspirational, accepting, supportive, and fun to work with. In that one day, she introduced us to the Myers-Briggs Personality Inventories and to Jack R. Gibbs' models of the development of a group (from his book *Trust and the Emotional Cycle of Change*).

After the discussion of Myers-Briggs, I felt I had a new vocabulary for understanding and accepting the differences among colleagues and students. For example, it turns out I am extremely introverted, intuitive, and judgmental, while my principal is extroverted, perceiving, and sensing. Because we now know we complement each other, we build on this as a strength. When I blue sky too much, Joanne asks me to *list* the steps and resources to make it happen.

This new knowledge was something to share with the whole faculty. (Indeed, we had Karen return in the spring to share her Myers-Briggs perspectives with the whole staff on another of our curriculum release days.)

What has meant the most to me, however, was Karen's presentation of the Gibbs' work on group development. Gibbs has identified a progression of stages that must occur for groups to function well together. If earlier stages are ignored, the trust building needed for success never materializes.

As Karen graphed out for us the transitions from Uninformed Optimism to Informed Pessimism, to Hopeful Realism, to Informed Optimism, and finally, to Rewarding Completion, we all had a good laugh. (See Change Reproducible 3.1.) We recognized that we as a school were currently stuck at stage two: Informed Pessimism. We knew now that we had an uphill

My Four Ts for Dealing with Change Transitions

TRUST
Build it; work it; don't neglect it.

TIME
Provide enough for *mastery* of new skills.

TRAINING
Continue until use and acceptance levels are high.

TOOLS
Provide to all learners to use in ways *they* learn best.

struggle ahead of us, requiring a great deal of energy, before we would make it over the plateau of hopeful realism.

What strikes me every time I review this information is the concern for inclusion at the beginning of the chain. There is a deep need for people to address the questions: "Who am I?", "Do I fit here?", and "What will I have to do?" It seems that if this need is not met, a backlash may set in that includes attitudes of cynicism and suspicion, conflict avoidance, making decisions for others, fear, and distrust. I also learned that all new members joining a group need to be allowed to go through the early stages to truly become part of the effort.

Forging Ahead

In a little over a month after this meeting with Karen Spencer, we were in the midst of a teachers' strike that closed the school for one week. There was such unity in our building that we returned to work the next week with fewer scars and difficulties than I had anticipated. Work-to-rule was over, and we could now forge ahead. In fact, one month later we had five committees that went to work on the priorities we had set the previous year.

Our program of reciprocal observations by colleagues was again funded and restarted with double the number of teams of the first year.

Two teachers were sent to a workshop on cooperative learning strategies. Our learning styles committee exchanged ideas and practices, and we soon had moved toward the Johnson and Johnson model of cooperative learning because of its focus on positive interdependence. Informally, we tried to implement these ideas in the classroom and share our successes and failures with each other. By year's end we knew that we wanted to continue together next year, but we wanted to know more about learning styles as they influenced the way our students learned in the classroom.

Our grouping/scheduling committee conducted several surveys. The first item we chose to tackle was our lunch cycle. We had three lunch periods of 22 minutes each and wanted to change this to two lunch periods of 30 minutes each. By May the proposals were in place and we had a trial run of the system on the day the fifth graders (next year's sixth graders) visited so that they could experience this, too. Staff and students were then polled to determine preferences for the three- or two-period systems. We had already hassled out in committee what numbers we felt we needed to say we had a mandate for change. We met this goal and the two-period lunch became a reality the next year.

By the way, we are back to three periods. Not because two failed, but because the enrollment grew just enough that we could not seat all the students in only two sessions. Was this a failure? Emphatically, no! The decisions were made by and for the community. We had established a process for introducing change that came from within the whole organization.

I should probably mention that somewhere along the line the steering committee agreed that we would act by faculty consensus only. We decided that we did not want to deal with the aftermath of win-lose decisions or the fact that colleagues who were on the losing side of an issue could sabotage change just by not following through with the agreements. Consensus took extra time, and many was the meeting when I wished we could just take a majority vote and get it over with, but as I look back, I'm glad we didn't.

Year Three

October of our third year in the Mastery-in-Learning Project saw the birth of the IBM-NEA MILPNET telecommunications network (now called the School Renewal Network). As one of the site coordinators for this network, I became very involved, first in learning how to use this system, and then in training other colleagues to use it.

The network focuses on school renewal and its related issues. It is not only a place for teachers, administrators, and parents from the participating schools to contact each other, it is also a place for researchers and facilitators to post research, dia-

logue with practitioners, test hypotheses, and pose pithy questions that continually ask us to reflect on our teaching practices.

As the initial trainer, I spent the most time with the system, conversed freely over the wires, and immediately felt as if the walls of my classroom had been blown away. Questions I did not feel comfortable asking my colleague next door I could ask of colleagues all across the country. I knew they would respond in an impartial manner. What an eye opener to hear about the events taking place in other schools across the U.S.!

I began to copy pertinent articles. I'd drop them in the principal's mailbox; I'd send articles to our superintendent; I'd send articles to colleagues who had expressed an in-

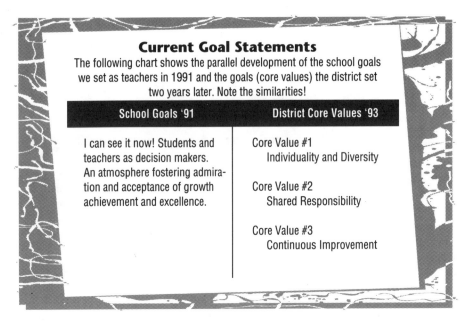

Current Goal Statements

The following chart shows the parallel development of the school goals we set as teachers in 1991 and the goals (core values) the district set two years later. Note the similarities!

School Goals '91	District Core Values '93
I can see it now! Students and teachers as decision makers. An atmosphere fostering admiration and acceptance of growth achievement and excellence.	Core Value #1 Individuality and Diversity Core Value #2 Shared Responsibility Core Value #3 Continuous Improvement

terest in these ideas. When questions arose, I could always pull something up through this system that was pertinent. We, as teachers, now had a source for rapid, reliable information on educational topics, and we began to use it. We also ran a tech fair for ourselves that first spring, with teachers sharing their computer expertise with each other in a round robin fashion.

Year three saw several other changes as well. The hardest to deal with was

the illness of our principal. As a staff, we "kept-on-keeping-on," but it was increasingly more stressful as the year progressed.

As in previous years, our committee had a hard time getting things going in the first semester. (Was a pattern developing to this process?) Once again, it was March when new things began to happen. At that time, the steering committee sponsored a curriculum release-day workshop on cooperative learning, followed later that spring by another workshop on learning styles. The consultant who presented this was available to work with individuals the next fall.

Also around this time, the construction of a new library for the school posed a new type of problem for us to handle. As soon as it became clear that the original library space could be converted into two classrooms, individuals started to request

I have never forgotten that moment of truly internalizing this view of change as a process with a life of its own.

these spaces. Interest exceeded the number of spaces. Instead of the principal just assigning people to the new space, he gave the issue to the steering committee to deal with. We formed an ad hoc committee (our first). This committee lasted for only six weeks, but is a model of what can go right. Everyone with any interest in the reallocation of any space within the building was invited. Attendance at the first meeting was almost half the staff. The beginning of the meeting was to me a nightmare as people began to say: " I want this space because.... I want that space because...." By the end of the meeting, it was a bit more calm because we chose to focus on two things: (1) make a master list of every possible available space and (2) define the educational needs of the different programs and the classes that were requesting these spaces. When we reconvened with the list of available spaces and wrote down the educational needs of programs, it was soon very easy for everyone around the table to begin creatively trading spaces to mutually benefit colleagues. The final list of proposals was taken to the full staff at our next meeting, and it was unanimously accepted.

That is not really the end of the story. Come June when people had to box up their classroom possessions for storage, and again in September when people got to move into their new spaces, there was no grumbling heard in the halls. Instead, in the spirit of cooperation, we were out there helping each other move and get settled because everyone was pleased with the space allocated.

There were additional benefits to this experience: We were able to allocate space for a teacher's workroom as well as two new conference rooms and a telephone room for all staff to use.

Year Four

In year four we had to dissolve our steering committee, form an official site-based management committee, and conform to the site-based management model conceived by school administrators and negotiated into our contract. I can't share much about this transition process because I was not elected to this new committee. As an observer, it seemed as if the same cycle of quiescent fall and winter, followed by a busy spring continued.

The major foci for the next few years were: revising our exploratory program, developing visionary goals for our school, and providing further training and implementation of learning styles-based teaching strategies.

Looking Back/ Looking Forward

We started eight years ago with only our profile and our "imagings." Thanks in part to the efforts of Ron Godfrey (who, after the appropriate training, became our in-house certified learning-styles trainer), you will see students throughout the school working in the corridor in addition to the classroom. On any given day, you can see drama in action; huge posters being constructed; students teaching and testing each other; and above all else, students excited about what they are doing and learning.

All space is viewed as instructional space. For example, my life science students use and maintain my large collection of living plants, which we house on the stairwell landing outside my classroom. This way, the collection is accessible to all and used by colleagues

If you had visited last March, you would have seen sixth graders involved in a totally peer-based science exhibition of original student experiments. (This idea has been partially adopted by our sister school across town.)

Last April you could have visited Arts Night and seen students perform original drama; read original poems, stories, and essays; or perform musical compositions. Or, you could have wandered the halls and read the writing samples on display from *every* student in the school.

Last June you could have seen the first ever math fair conducted by one of our eighth grade teams. This year it may be across the entire grade. The seventh grade teams are actively planning some type of interdisciplinary exhibition activity to take place in the spring.

As I reflect on how instructional practices that enhance learning for all of us are entering Diamond's classrooms at an accelerating pace, I feel proud to be part of these seasons of change.

Early on at Scanticon, I happened to pick up a small spiral-bound book of sayings meant for business people entitled *The Best of Success*. One saying seems particularly pertinent:

The purpose of goals is to focus our attention. The mind will not reach toward achievement until it has clear objectives. The magic begins when we set goals. It is then that the switch is turned on, the current begins to flow, and the power to accomplish becomes reality.

My final advice to teachers engaged in change is to set your goals wisely, permit yourself to go slowly, and don't forget to look back every so often. One of those times you just might be surprised to realize how far you have come! ◆

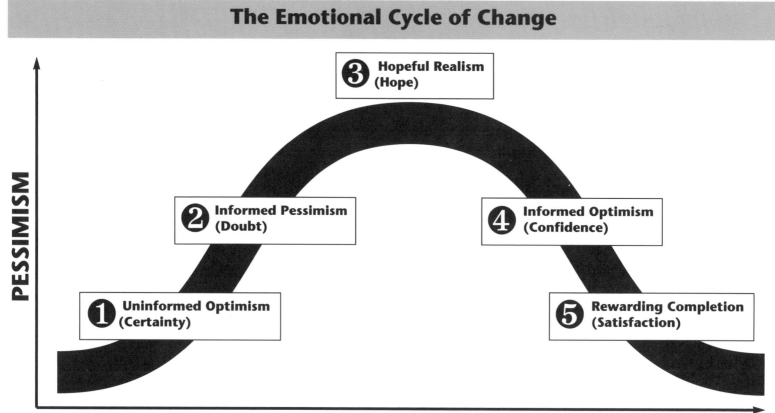

The Emotional Cycle of Change

PESSIMISM

3 **Hopeful Realism**
(Hope)

2 **Informed Pessimism**
(Doubt)

4 **Informed Optimism**
(Confidence)

1 **Uninformed Optimism**
(Certainty)

5 **Rewarding Completion**
(Satisfaction)

TIME

Source: "The Emotional Cycle of Change," by Don Kelley and Daryl R. Conner. In *The 1979 Annual Handbook for Group Facilitators.* La Jolla, Calif.: University Associates.

Reader Reflections

Insights: _____

_____

_____

_____

_____

_____

Actions for Our School (District) to Consider: _____

_____

_____

_____

_____

_____

_____

_____

_____

BRINGING A NEW ORDER TO THINGS

Our inquiry group system has restructured school time to provide for school-based research and faculty collaboration.

4

There is nothing more difficult to take in hand, more perilous to conduct, or more uncertain in its success, than to take the lead in the introduction of a new order of things.
—Machiavelli

Just a few years ago, I was an international underwriter and political risk specialist for Chubb and Son, Inc. In 1991 I decided that I wanted to work harder and make less money, so I enrolled in a teacher-education pro-gram. In 1992 I completed the University of Maryland's Master's Certification Program and received my teaching certification.

Finally, in 1993 I became "a critical force for change." I became a fifth grade teacher at Jackson Road Elementary School in the Montgomery County Public School system in Maryland.

My school is a Chapter 1 school that teaches 60 percent minority. students. Students in my classroom speak four languages and take everything from Ritalin to Flintstones Chewables. The children are wonderful, but many come to school looking for the boundaries that no one else is willing to provide for them. I love my job (I even have a sign that my mentor teacher made for me during student teaching that says so!), yet I know that the person who has my old job is making $20,000 more per year before bonuses, stock options, and 401Ks with matching funds (and he gets to go to the bathroom whenever he wants). But who am I kidding? I didn't choose teaching; it chose me.

I did, however, choose my school and one of the reasons I did so was because of our inquiry-group system, a way our staff has restructured school time to provide for faculty collaboration and

JONATHAN C. KIEFFER

Fifth Grade Teacher
Jackson Road Elementary School
Montgomery County Public Schools, Maryland

school-based research.

I found out about my current school during my graduate program, when John O'Flahavan, one of my professors, told me he was creating a model School Research Center (SRC) that would be a vital part of Jackson Road Elementary School (JRES).

The SRC Program

Located within the school, the SRC program

Through inquiry groups, you become a part of something bigger than your classroom.

now uses teacher research to develop and test solutions to the problems we teachers face in today's public schools.

The program is best described as a joint venture that merges the resources of Jackson Road Elementary, the College of Education (University of Maryland-College Park), and the National Reading Research Center (NRRC). It's current mission statement is to wed:

field-based teacher education and teacher research into one coherent program for the purpose of aligning teaching with the needs of students who are at risk of academic failure—especially in areas of literacy and numeracy.

In other words, we at JRES are looking for ways to do our job better. We have the necessary resources at our disposal to do it and a sensible approach—site-based teacher research. Why did we choose site-based teacher

research? Because we already know that "fix-all" directives from above simply cannot, and will not, satisfy the needs of a society as diverse as ours. You cannot be all things to all people all the time. Business realized this "market niche" reality years ago. We believe it's time that education realizes the same thing and starts satisfying the needs of its local market niches. As business has learned, this can only be accomplished through local market research, for us—teacher research.

What Are Inquiry Groups?

Much of our teacher research originates from *inquiry groups*, groups of teachers from our school (plus, a researcher and an administrator or two) who get together to discuss the

problems and needs they encounter in their everyday teaching. As a group, these educators discuss problematic situations, pose and test solutions, and draw conclusions from the results.

One time I explained this inquiry-group concept to a lay friend of mine, and he made this comment:

Teachers are like woodcutters who are so busy chopping wood that they never have time to sharpen their ax. This joint venture allows you to sharpen your ax.

I couldn't have agreed more. It seems business has long encouraged employees to take time to sharpen their ax. Education, however, encourages employees to just hit the wood harder and more often. But at JRES, it's different.

A Typical Inquiry Group Meeting

Let me walk you through a typical inquiry-group meeting, which by the way, is conducted approximately once a month for three to three and one-half hours.

You walk into the teacher's room, check your messages, get a cup of coffee, sit down at a big table, look over your notes from the last meeting, look over what you want to discuss today, and talk to your colleagues as you wait for everyone to get settled. You can even go to the bathroom if you want to.

Seated with you (say you are a fifth grade teacher like me) are nine other teachers: a special education/resource teacher; a kindergarten, first grade, second grade, and fifth grade teacher; the media specialist; a student teacher; the principal (for part of the meeting, if desired); and a college professor who supports teacher research and school-based change.

The professor moderates the beginning of the meeting. Each teacher has about 20 minutes to discuss his or her issues; colleagues offer suggestions or comments; and the professor mentions research already completed on the topic.

As the meeting progresses, plans of action are developed, "see me later" notes are passed around, schedules are checked, people move to other rooms or to the side to discuss an idea further, and the professor takes a break from a quick discussion to say that abstracts from the meeting will be in your box within a week or so. Slowly, the room empties.

If it was an a.m. meeting, you go to lunch or back to your room to look over the lesson plans or notes the student teacher, who was responsible for your class during the meeting, left you. You are excited; you have ideas to improve your craft; and you know that you are a part of something bigger than your classroom. If it was a p.m. meeting, you go home.

Inquiry Groups Empower Teachers

I believe our inquiry groups empower teachers by reminding them that they are part of a team that can help them improve their craft.

A simple example: At my first meeting, Karen, a second grade teacher, said that she had a new student in her room who spoke only Russian. She needed to know if he, Stephen, knew how to read. She didn't know when the county would see him, and she was frustrated. It was my third week at JRES, and no one knew that I studied Russian in college. If not for the inquiry groups, no one may have ever known.

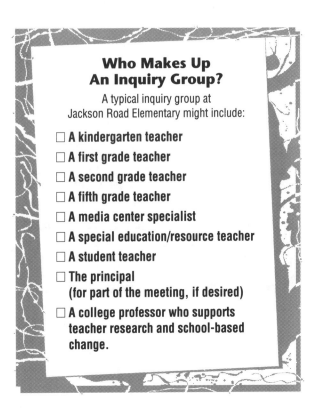

Who Makes Up An Inquiry Group?

A typical inquiry group at Jackson Road Elementary might include:

☐ **A kindergarten teacher**

☐ **A first grade teacher**

☐ **A second grade teacher**

☐ **A fifth grade teacher**

☐ **A media center specialist**

☐ **A special education/resource teacher**

☐ **A student teacher**

☐ **The principal (for part of the meeting, if desired)**

☐ **A college professor who supports teacher research and school-based change.**

The next day, I went to her class during my planning period to speak with guage (ESL) students. And, more important, I had established an open

Business has long encouraged employees to take time to sharpen their ax. Education, however, encourages employees to just hit the wood harder and more often.

Stephen. I brought a simple Russian book. We talked for a little bit. Ten minutes later, she knew that the child had not been taught how to read. While I was there, however, I had an opportunity to talk with the student teacher in that room. We talked about what she had been doing with Stephen. I was fascinated.

When I went back to my class, I had some ideas for working with my own English as a Second Lan-

dialogue with two research professionals on the other side of the building. You know that's tough to do when you've only been teaching three weeks. It's even tougher to do if you've been teaching 300 weeks. But inquiry groups provide a natural medium for open dialogue.

Sometimes that dialogue can become quite open. I remember my first inquiry group meeting where John told a teacher

that "maybe your kids are learning in spite of what you are doing, and not because of it." Tough comment. If I had not been through a program where that was basically the motto, I might have been as defensive as the teacher he addressed. But then John discussed the research conducted in that area and forced the teacher to really reflect on what she was doing. The outcome? We realized that the kids were learning because of what she was doing, but with some small adaptations, they could learn even more.

Inquiry Groups Foster Innovation

At times, adapting our teaching to the needs of the students has led our school into some risky and challenging ventures. The new fifth grade read-

ing program is one of the more aggressive ones.

Currently, almost 20 percent of the fifth grade is coded for what has traditionally been pullout reading-resource help. This year, while examining the program within our inquiry groups, we decided to break the resource teacher/pullout paradigm. Instead of having the children pulled out, we're having two of the resource teachers pulled in.

For example, at the fifth grade level, there are three classroom teachers, and we are departmentalized for social studies, science, and mathematics, although instruction crosses over as much as possible via interdisciplinary projects. Last year, students were pulled out during the day for 20 minutes of reading help here or there.

This year, however, we are implementing a variation of the Joplin Plan (Good and Brophy, 1991).

In the afternoon, during a scheduled reading class, each resource teacher takes the children that are assigned to her. Their classes are about 10 students each, while the regular classroom teacher has about 16 students. For one hour, four days a week, all students receive intense, individualized reading instruction. The classes are still heterogeneous, but in a way that the numbers allow more personal interaction for a greater number of students. Plus, the former pullout students no longer miss valuable instruction in other subjects.

The plan required some rescheduling and an extra classroom, but the resource teachers are now accountable for the entire planning and reading grade for their old pullouts. They are also considered part of a team that is working to find ways of improving reading instruction for all students.

Some parents were a little anxious about their children going to the school "resource" teacher. When we told them, however, that it was their "reading" teacher and that the approach allowed smaller class sizes and more individualized attention, they supported it. The program also places kids with different friends than those in their heterogeneous homerooms, with whom they travel the rest of the day. Because the program began with teachers, we can change the program, switch the kids, and adapt the strategies as we need to in order to satisfy our goals of literacy.

Benefits to Student Teachers

Let's talk more about student teachers and their role in inquiry groups. At our school, we also have shattered the student-teacher paradigm (we're into paradigm breaking).

Student teachers do not stick with one supervising teacher day in and day out. Each student teacher gets the opportunity to plan lessons for and teach all grade levels and abilities, from gifted and talented to learning disabled and special education. Our objective is to expose each student teacher to a variety of curriculums, grouping strategies, seating arrangements, room procedures, teaching styles, and teacher personalities.

Student teachers are viewed as part of the team and as such, they sit in on inquiry group meetings. But their schedules are arranged so that they also cover for teachers during inquiry group meetings they are not part of. Often, that means student teachers will cover a class they are not currently teaching. In these cases, classroom

An inquiry-group meeting is not time away from the kids; it is time invested in them.

teachers discuss what their students are studying with the student teachers, who, in turn, plan a lesson. So far, the arrangement has worked very well.

Implementing Inquiry Groups

Implementing inquiry groups does have its share of challenges, and I wouldn't be telling "the whole story" if I didn't elaborate on these.

First, there are the scheduling challenges. Every time we're due for a meeting, our principal and John have to schedule two different inquiry-group meetings, making sure that: (1) teachers don't lose planning time,

Teaching is simply too complex and exhausting for one person to do it alone.

(2) there is a student teacher and coverage for each teacher-researcher, and (3) the inquiry groups are representative of the resources in the school.

Then there's the teacher buy-in aspect. Teachers have to buy into the fact that these meetings are not in addition to other responsibilities, but a complement to them. In other words, this is not time away from the kids; it is time invested in them.

I am finding that teachers are so concerned about time away from their kids that they are neglecting their "selves." I realize that delegation comes hard to teachers in matters concerned with "their kids," but the job is simply too complex and exhausting for one person to do it alone, without time for team reflection. Isolation does not have to be a part of the job, but only teachers can change that. Involving teachers in research helps avoid that isolation.

Plus, the teacher research component of our inquiry groups encourages the reflection time we need. Coming from busi-ness, I believe I was more willing to accept and able to appreciate this priori-tizing of responsibilities. Unfortunately, those who have been in education longer than I, have be-come conditioned to emp-ty initiatives. I respect their doubts. But our arrangement is not empty because it is initiated by the school, not in addition to it. The program is structured to remind teachers of that reality.

I have a story: When the student teacher as-signed to cover my class tracked me down at lunch duty to ask me about what I was teaching, I had no problem giving her the re-sponsibility. When we finished, I said that I was sorry I didn't talk to her sooner. She just looked at me and said, "Hey, that's my job."

It was her job, and she had been selected by John because she could do the job without additional teacher assistance. Some-times the student teachers did a better job than I would have done. Other times, they didn't. Either way, it was only one day out of some 180. Teachers have to keep this perspec-tive if they hope to main-tain their sanity in this impossible job under im-possible conditions.

How Are We Doing? Where Are We Going?

The JRES-SRC program is only in its second year, and the plans and possi-bilities continue to ex-pand. We have scheduled education experts in spe-cific areas to come to school and assist teachers in implementing new strategies. For example, two doctoral students will soon be assisting teachers with literature circles.

Another resource addition is our new half-time kindergarten teacher. She is currently attending the University of Maryland for her master's degree and is part-time teacher, part-time graduate/research assistant to be used by the "teacher researchers" at Jackson Road.

Resources are the key to any school-improvement program, and we have them. The one complaint John relayed to us from the student teachers of the previous year is that they wished they had been used more often as resources for practicing teachers.

This year there are also research stipends available to teachers to assist them in their research. The goal is to have teach-ers more involved with research that enables them to mesh their personal goals with the institutional goals of the school (O'Flahavan 1993).

On the whole, the teachers at JRES have an *esprit de corps* that is exciting to see and even more exciting to be a part of. Whether it's helping a nonEnglish-speaking child adjust to second grade or designing an effective reading pullout program, JRES is looking for ways to "do the right thing."

A final comment and cautionary note before I conclude: "Doing the right thing" can evolve quickly into "doing too much of the right thing." During our second year with the inquiry groups, we became so involved with our research and so excited about our opportuni-ties that the inquiry groups started to control us instead of the other way around. We were doing too much, too fast. One teammate summed it up this way: "We are so afraid that we won't get these opportunities again that we are running ourselves ragged."

My warning is this: In all likelihood, you will overextend yourselves. This will happen not because something is wrong, but because something is going so right that you want more. Your time, however, is finite. When this realization rears its angry head, remember that you set this up, and that you can change it. Don't expect to cross all your t's and dot all your i's the first time you attempt a program such as this. The ideas are what is important. To paraphrase one teammate: "In a rough draft, spelling doesn't count."

In my opinion, there is no better way to find the answers to today's educational dilemmas than through teacher research. It can help us bring a new order to things. Granted such endeavors take time and a lot of hard work, but it is time and energy well spent. ◆

Start Your Own Inquiry Groups

1 Gather a critical mass at your school that wants to pursue the formation of inquiry groups and/or whatever they may lead to.

2 Find or choose a coordinator to be responsible for implementing and developing the program. For lack of a better phrase: "Someone has to be in charge." It can be a teacher, but be prepared to adapt that person's schedule so he or she can devote time to your endeavor.

3 Read the articles listed at the end of this book and begin defining your needs. Follow up on the resources you find.

4 Contact the education department of a local university who is either conducting research in the schools in your area or is looking to begin research in your area. Drag these educators out of their ivory towers and invite them to the true research facilities!

5 Contact a student-teacher coordinator and present your and the university's ideas and needs.

6 Rough out the logistics of what you will need regarding number of teacher participants, student teachers, university staff, and so on in order to establish inquiry groups in your school.

7 Report to faculty members on your progress and then make them aware of the program needs and limitations, as defined to you by your partners—the university and student teacher programs.

8 Answer the question: Do we, as a school, still want to do this?

9 Get the OK from whomever it is in your district that gives OKs.

10 Set up schedules and go for it.

Reader Reflections

Insights: _____

_____

_____

_____

_____

_____

Actions for Our School (District) to Consider: _____

_____

_____

_____

_____

_____

_____

_____

PUSHING LEARNING BEYOND THE CLASSROOM WALLS

Teachers in this school district learned to use Outcome-Based Education to better prepare students for living in the real world.

5

As a veteran classroom teacher, I've experienced lots of frustrations, as I'm sure all of you who are reading this have. Frustration has become "the nature of the beast," it seems, in our quest to meet increasing expectations of a changing, complex world. Our students' futures are in our hands.

So, day after day, we work like mad, doing our small bit to get kids prepared to lead productive lives beyond the classroom. This is no

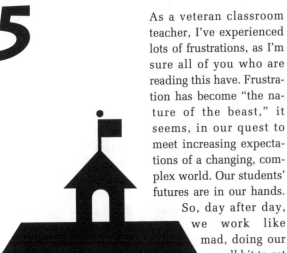

doubt as true for you as it is for me.

Investigating the World Beyond the Classroom

I work in a small upstate suburban community not far from Rochester, called Macedon, and teach in the Richard Mann Building of the Gananda Community School District. Two years ago, I was feeling this

JEANNE LOKAR

Fifth Grade Teacher

Richard Mann Building

Gananda Community School District

Macedon, New York

frustration I spoke of as I was working with (at?) a group of my fifth graders on mastering the complexities of writing a business letter. "Why do we need to know this stuff?" came the question from a student. Rather than offer the pathetic rationale: "It's part of the curriculum," I was quick to point out that we'd be using this newly acquired skill to write to real businesses to share our real consumer concerns.

So began Power of the Pen, a year-long effort whereby my students would write to a wide variety of local and national businesses to offer complaints, compliments, or questions on products and services with which they had personal experience. The world beyond the classroom easily became our domain. As each child wrote and then sent letters to businesses, responses and changes came rapidly. What we were doing in school involved *real life*. Everything from receiving free samples to being the impetus for policy change in a company became the result of my students writing effective letters.

With this small venture touching the world beyond the classroom walls, I began to see learning in a broader arena. In the

"Knowing something" is almost meaningless unless what we know can be put to use in a meaningful way, in a real-life context.

faculty room and in other casual conversations with colleagues and my principal, Emma Klimek, we began a dialogue about how we could push everyday learning beyond the classroom walls. Ideas abounded.

Mrs. Klimek shared with me some of her knowledge of Outcome-Based Education (OBE), that she had acquired at a national conference provided by the High Success Network (and led by William Spady), in Colorado. OBE is based on developing specific, real-world ends that a school wants to accomplish for all students. These in turn are used to develop program goals, course goals, and unit and lesson outcomes.

The more I heard, the more excited I became. Mrs. Klimek assured me that much of what I'd been doing for years with kids was really OBE in nature. With that reassurance, and her encouragement, I began to learn about Outcome-Based Education.

As part of this process, I, along with my friend and colleague, second grade teacher Pam Wesley, traveled to Colorado for a week-long training session on OBE. Being surrounded with other teachers and led by the experts (Bill Spady, Kit Marshall, Spence Rogers) I had one "eureka moment" after another!

Over the week's training, my learning led me to see how I could eliminate much of the dreaded frustration I'd been feeling by embracing the OBE philosophy. I found out that I didn't have to throw out the "baby with the bath water" to better prepare kids for the future. I just had to refocus and restructure things a bit. I was thrilled and ready to begin to make some changes.

Learning More About OBE

Developing a true understanding of Outcome-Based Education philosophy took time. It is complex, yet common sense. I read lots and talked to everyone who knew anything about it. Like a puzzle, there were many interrelated pieces that needed to be put together to create the final picture. That required hard work and could be very frustrating at times.

My principal was, and continues to be, a real support, providing information and encouragement. But that doesn't mean she didn't have her own moments of doubt.

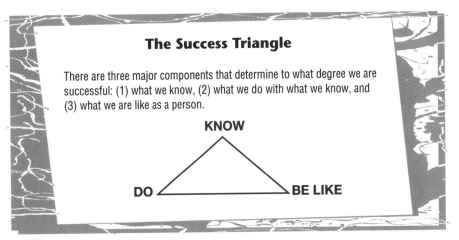

The Success Triangle

There are three major components that determine to what degree we are successful: (1) what we know, (2) what we do with what we know, and (3) what we are like as a person.

During our first ventures into OBE, she often shared with our staff her concern that, "we're on a fast train, but may be on the wrong track," so I knew that she was feeling the same frustration that I was (though from a different vantage point).

A skeptic by nature, I tried again and again to punch holes in the OBE philosophy. It was a personal revelation that solidified my commitment to examining the need for change in our schools: I have two grown daughters. One daughter did mediocre work in school and got poor grades. As an adult, she is an achiever and functions well as a contributing member of the community. The other daughter was an academic star, yet "can't do life." I asked myself, "What's wrong with this pic-ture??!!" Shouldn't suc-cess in school be directly correlated with success in real life? If not, *why* are we doing *what* we're do-ing?

My personal quest for an answer, and for change, grew. I became more committed to under-standing and implement-ing OBE. It simply made sense.

Kit Marshall of the High Success Network explains the "success triangle (see diagram, this page)." Let's accept the fact that there are three major compo-nents that determine to what degree we are suc-cessful in our lives:

1. What we know. (cog-nition)

2. What we do with what we know. (compe-tence)

3. What we are like as a person. (orientation)

Historically, our strong-est educational focus, by far, has been on one of the triangle's points: What we know.... the content/ information "stuff" that we try desperately to pour into children's minds, hoping this becomes the tool for them to use to build a future. If we take a look at our own adult lives and successes we've had along the way, we see that the knowledge we bring to any situation (job, relationships, hobbies, etc.) plays only a small part in bringing us to the point of success.

Developing a true un-derstanding and apprecia-tion of the success trian-gle really helped me to shift my teaching focus. "Knowing something" is almost meaningless un-less what we know can be put to use in a meaningful way, in a real-life context. And, along the way, the development of personali-ty and character must be addressed and nurtured.

There are four princi-ples of OBE that act as a model:

1. Design Down; Deliv-er Up: Like planning a trip, we must decide first where we want to end up (significant outcomes), then make the plan for how to get there.

2. High Expectations and Standards: We must be direct and specific about the quality of work that's expected.

3. Clarity of Focus: We must decide what we want kids to get from each activity/unit/performance. Is it clear to you? Is it clear to them?

4. Expanded Opportunities: It is also crucial to provide repeated chances for a student to succeed at a given task.

Parallel to these principles are the three premis-

... along the way, the development of personality and character must be addressed and nurtured.

es of Outcome-Based Education, or the basics of its belief system. They are:

1. All students can learn (though not in the same way and at the same time).

2. Success breeds success (just as failure breeds failure).

3. We control the conditions of success (no use looking for someone else to take responsibility).

Making Change Happen

After much education on the topic of Outcome-Based Education, Pam and I began to feel a solid commitment toward making some schoolwide changes.

How could we do that? The first step was to take a look at our staff and students and community. Two questions guided us: What changes do we need to make? How can we do it? Once again, we reflected on the success triangle: We needed knowledge, we needed to provide a

supportive environment for putting that knowledge to use, and we needed to have people commit to making some changes.

Change is a scary thing for all of us. Fighting the "but we've always done it this way" mentality is an uphill battle. Nowhere is this more true than in education. Change is a slow process, not a one-time event.

Pam and I worked to put together an after-school workshop for our faculty on the topic of *Change* (subtitled "Only a Baby Likes a Change").

In casual conversations over the weeks we'd become involved in OBE, we had shared our excitement and ideas with fellow teachers, and the principal spoke often about the need to move toward a more future-oriented education system

for the students in our charge. So when Pam and I offered the voluntary workshop, we had lots of takers.

We talked to our fellow teachers about the phases of change, based on those we had so recently experienced. Initial feelings of confusion led to information gathering, then to acceptance of the need for change, and finally to identifying how to make personal and professional changes. We conducted an open dialogue with our colleagues, and because Pam and I had begun to establish ourselves as leaders in the OBE movement, we worked to identify problem areas (resistance) as well as changes we had made in our own classrooms (application).

Our faculty is small and close-knit and progressive by nature, so we were lucky to have most of our peers show enthusiasm toward the change process and the move toward creation of Outcome-Based Education in our K-5 school.

So often, change in schools begins with the existing curriculum: It's the familiar. Probably our biggest challenge is to have educators begin a dialogue that addresses the question: "What do we want our students to know, do, and be like when they leave school?" Working toward the answer forces us through the painful process of deciding what, in our existing curriculum, we should keep, what should be altered, and what should be eliminated. Sounds easy. It's not. But without this critical step, we won't arrive at what we want: *significant outcomes.*

How this process gets done varies from school to school, depending on many factors: staff size, level of interest, time available. In my small district, the principal and a few of us who had expressed an interest, began the work, later to be joined by others. We knew that if we could publicize our classroom successes, others would follow. It became our very own Field of Dreams!

Among ourselves, we talked about the three premises of OBE. Clearly, we shared these beliefs. Next, we examined the four principles and how each could manifest itself in our various classrooms. For months, we shared small successes and encouraged steps toward outcome-based learning. In our leadership roles, Pam and I were always on

the lookout for classroom experiences that had an OBE bent. Each discovery was publicized and celebrated. We knew that success breeds success in *all* of us, not only our students. Some examples:

• Pam's second graders had always experienced a careers unit, complete with worksheets. With OBE as a guide, Pam now has each student setting up, conducting, and reporting to the class on a person interviewed from the child's career-choice field.

• The first grade teachers had talked lots to the children about the environment, but the current extension of that in-class discussion is a school-wide recycling and composting effort.

• In fifth grade, we discuss the need to be educated consumers. Where

worksheets were once the core of the children's work, we now have a fully operational, profit-generating school store, complete with all the math, language arts, and social skills needed to run a small business.

Growing in Commitment

With each change, our commitment to Outcome-Based Education has grown. Parents and the larger community have taken an active role. As the community saw the excitement of the children and beyond-the-classroom evidence of the learning, parents began to show an eagerness to become involved. Our PTA has become revitalized, helping to provide some volunteer people-power when more

continue to broaden our understanding through reading, research, and networking.

The High Success Network is the organization that has been by far the key to unlocking the mystery. This group of experts continues to be on the cutting edge of educational change. The various

ings, through mini-workshops, and by dropping pertinent print information into teachers' mailboxes. We even invite experts in to speak on OBE; this helps us all and adds credibility to the movement.

Outcome-Based Education has given us a shot in the arm. Frustration may continue to be a part of our work with children. But, as we move toward the future, and a school system that truly prepares our young people to embrace it, it's the overriding sense of accomplishment and success that motivates us all to continue to move forward. As we move toward the twenty-first century, we now know that we are on the right track. ◆

Change is a very scary thing for all of us. Fighting the "but we've always done it this way" mentality is an uphill battle.

hands are needed.

As I said earlier, Outcome-Based Education is complex. Like peeling an onion, there are layers to uncover and new dimensions to understand and experience. Pam and I

materials and services they provide were, at the beginning, and continue to be, invaluable. We disseminate information as we get it to our colleagues: in casual conversations, at faculty meet-

Change Maker's Primer

Starting Points for Instructional Change	Getting Through the Changes Ahead
✓ Cooperative learning ✓ Authentic assessment ✓ Writing process ✓ Rubrics ✓ Portfolios ✓ Whole language ✓ Effective schools program ✓ Integrated curriculum ✓ Teaming	1. Recognize the need for change. 2. Work smarter, not harder. 3. Decide what's important. Choose your battles wisely. 4. Make the best of your personal strengths/interests.

Components of School Change

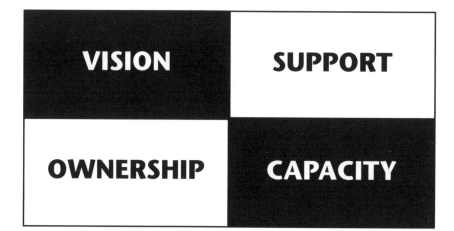

OBE Curriculum Is:

- **Designed down, delivered up**
  - **Driven by exit outcomes**
    - **For all students**
      - **Focused on learning for an authentic audience**
        - **Assessed by outcome through performance**

Curriculum Comparison

Traditional Curriculum	OBE Curriculum
Time-based	Outcomes-based
Sequential	Nonsequential
Focused on content	Focused on real-life issues
Aligned with textbooks or standardized tests	Aligned with outcomes
Tracked	Not tracked
Assessed by course	Assessed by outcomes

The OBE Model

Curriculum Content and Structure		**Instructional Delivery**
	OUTCOMES (exit)	
Student Assessment and Credentialling		**Student Placement and Advancement**

Source: William Spady

Reader Reflections

Insights: _____

_____

_____

_____

_____

Actions for Our School (District) to Consider: _____

_____

_____

_____

_____

_____

_____

Outcome-Based Education is complex.
Like peeling an onion, there are layers to uncover and new dimensions
to understand and experience.

RISING FROM THE ASHES

My story is of school change, or to put it more accurately, of failure to initiate a school change and of the growth process that resulted from it.

6

In sitting down to write this, I was somewhat relieved to unload the feelings of anger and resentment that lay heavily upon my chest since a cold, snowy night last February (1992). This was the evening that a group of teachers in Seneca Falls, New York, advanced an idea for providing middle school students with an extra-help period, and in the process, was publicly "ambushed" by an ad hoc group of local parents. In doing research for and in writing this piece, much of my anger and resentment have disappeared. I have come to realize that some growth has been made since that snowy night. Change gets into people's comfort zones, simply stated.

The Story Begins

Please allow me to introduce myself. My name is Mike Marriam and I am entering my twentieth year of teaching, with 17 of those years at the middle levels of public education. I entered teaching to experience the richness of working with young people. I have been fortunate enough to teach middle school reading in a community I have grown to love; I enjoy the students that I work with; and I feel I am a part of a great faculty, one that has treated me like a member of a large family since I came to this district 15 years ago.

Seneca Falls, is a small, rural community of around 7,000 residents, located between Syracuse and Rochester, in the heart of the Finger Lakes region. It is one of those small towns where everybody is usually united by the local manufacturing concern (in this case, Goulds Pumps, Inc.) or by mention of whichever high school sports team is currently the hottest.

MIKE MARRIAM

Reading Teacher
Seneca Middle School
Seneca Falls, New York

Seneca Falls once boasted of a rich academic tradition, but the local demographics have changed greatly in the 15 years that I have been here. One major manufacturing concern relocated its management staff and operations to the midwest, the local hospi-

If vocal factions of the community were asking us to become accountable as teachers, then we must also become responsible for our teaching conditions.

tal is gone, and the Seneca Falls Army Depot has been de-emphasized.

Changing demographics and its accompanying economic effects have been reflected in the school district as well. We had to close one elementary building five years ago, forcing us to change our district configuration and leading us to decide to transform our junior high (grades seven through nine) into a middle school (grades five through eight).

The Seneca Middle School, established in the fall of 1988, had some rather unique characteristics. Physically, we were attached to our high school, Mynderse Academy, divided only by a set of steel doors. Our school population numbered from about 110 to 130 or so students per grade level with a core team of teachers for each grade level that consists of one each from the English, science, social studies, and math disciplines. Noncore "special area" courses (art,

home economics, health, technology, and foreign languages) were taught by teachers responsible for classes in both of the buildings (these teachers were called "crossovers" in Seneca Middle School jargon).

The schedules for both the middle and high school staff were identical in beginning and ending times, and the 40-minute duration of instructional periods. Teachers in both buildings started at 7:55 a.m. and concluded the day at 3:15 p.m. While high school classes began at 8 o'clock, the middle school was conducting its daily team meetings. Students arrived at school around 8:30 and began classes at around 8:44 (just as the high school was beginning its second period). The high school finished classes at 2:30,

with extra help, detention, and meeting time from 2:30 to 3:15 (tenth period). The middle school, starting one period later, concluded its instructional day at 3:15, with no extra-help time.

Parents of the middle school students felt that the staggered schedule would isolate younger students from older high school students on bus runs, preventing the possibility of negative social interaction. It also allowed any of the special area teachers to attend the middle school's daily team meetings and help in decision making. Seventh and eighth grade students participating in band and chorus programs began these activities at 7:55 a.m., eliminating a scheduling logjam during the school day. In the fall of 1988, we were of the opinion that Seneca Falls had the distinction of having the only middle school that incorporated special area teachers in the teaming process. We began the school year full of hope and enthusiasm.

The Problem

Yet, the very features that we set in place to define our middle school soon became problematic. Crossover teachers often found that they had to teach a class in one building, then hustle through the steel doors to get to the next class in the other building on time. This also forced our entire middle school to keep our instructional schedule parallel with that of the high school. Because of this arrangement, we discovered that it was impossible to develop flexible time frames in the middle

school that appeared in exemplary programs, such as block scheduling, minicourses, and extra learning times for students. Middle school students needing extra instruction outside of their 40-minute class or other personal time with teachers found that it could not fit into the school day.

The Proposal

Near the conclusion of the 1991-92 school year, eighth grade teachers Nancy Pearse (French and Spanish) and Ron Fleury (math) asked if our starting and ending times for students could coincide with those of the high school so that middle school students could receive extra help from 2:30-3:15. Core course teachers as well as many of the crossover teachers found that they needed

the extra period to work with students who had been absent or needed extra help. Synchronizing the two buildings' schedules so that extra-help time was automatically built into the end of the day seemed like the best option.

Eighth grade science teacher Lee Foster explained his personal reason for supporting the idea: "Lab work in our class is hands-on. If a student is absent, there is often no way to recreate that experience. The advantage would be that students would have an opportunity to come in and actually make up the lab or witness the demonstrations. That aspect is currently lost for absentees. Currently, students are given data and told to write up the conclusions. Tenth period would give

those students more options."

Nancy Pearse brought up the problems of the teacher who travels between schools. "I'm a crossover who teaches tenth period in the middle school. I can't give extra help to students in either building because of the present schedule. What am I to do?"

The flip side was that if the proposed schedule change were adopted, our students would arrive earlier (at the same time as the high school kids), eliminating the morning band/chorus program and possibly eliminating the special area teachers from participating in teaming.

Pearse and Fleury surveyed the middle school teachers to see if others would support a schedule change. Many teachers were interested, so they gave the results to the principal as an information document, with the idea of presenting a proposal to the Middle School Steering Committee. (This is a parent-teacher policymaking group. According to its

If administrative directives and decrees do not lead to the internalization of change by staff, then it is up to staff members to begin to initiate change themselves.

bylaws, it must have a parent-teacher ratio of approximately 2 to 1.)

At the meeting, Pearse and Fleury presented the committee with a list of pros and cons. Because the related change in bus scheduling affected the community, the committee decided to table the proposal until the district could gather further information. The proposal was postponed until the following school year.

Early in the 1992-93 school year, the idea began to gather momentum again. This time, the proposal to change the schedule for students had even more support from the faculty. In November, the principal distributed a formal survey to the staff. The survey listed advantages and disadvantages by departments and asked each member where he or she stood on the issue.

The vote was 23-3 in favor of the change, with the few teachers who cast abstentions willing to go along with the majority opinion on the issue.

The next logical step was to present the idea to the steering committee again. However, a parent information session was added to the agenda in which steering committee members presented the plan to any concerned parents. On that evening in early February, an unexpected number of people showed up, forcing the gathering from our middle school library to the more spacious high school cafeteria. Once the meeting got underway, it appeared that public opinion stood adamant on killing the proposal. Parent comments such as "teachers are lazy and want to go home at 2:30," "our shower schedules will have to change," and so on, were voiced. Remarks in opposition to the proposal were cheered.

Because the steering committee had called this gathering, we teachers who were present didn't think the rules of engagement allowed us to voice our support for the proposal, nor to defend ourselves from the unfounded charges of some parents. Those who supported the proposal were few in number.

The steering committee's decision a week later appeared to be a formality. (Remember: The committee has an approximate parent-to-teacher ratio of 2 to 1.) Buoyed by the parent forum of the preceding week, the committee's vote came to only 6-13 to support the proposed schedule change. Realizing that reaching a consensus was out of the question, our faculty representative, Ed Passifione, dropped the proposal.

The Aftermath

I digress from my story for a minute. I don't want to give the impression that the parent information session did not produce emotional casualties. Those of us present left with an empty feeling toward ownership of the change process in our school. Others felt that deliberate blocking tactics were employed.

In his book, *Making Schools Better: How Parents and Teachers Across the Country Are Taking Action — And You Can, Too,* author Larry Martz focuses on the "Hawthorne Effect." The term is derived from a research experiment in the late 1920s and early '30s in which conditions were improved for some factory workers at the Hawthorne Works of Western Electric in Cicero, Illinois (hence, the name). As the researchers anticipated, the productivity of the involved workers increased dramatically. But after the papers and instruments were packed, the researchers gone, and the conditions returned to the status quo, a strange phenomenon occurred. The level of productivity at the plant for the involved workers remained 25 percent above their pre-improvement average, causing the researchers to do follow-up studies. The researchers concluded that the very act of change itself induced the higher productivity, and the ownership of that change had a lasting effect on the selected workers.

The rest of Martz's book covers reforms that some of America's schools have accomplished and how each project has had a Hawthrone Effect on that school and its community.

I believe a reverse Hawthorne Effect could also be possible. Failure to achieve a desired change (such as our extra-help period) could have a negative impact on teacher morale and subsequent efforts to work for future change.

From the point of view of psychologists, conflict resolution is discussed in terms of "win-win" or "win-lose." Married couples understand this when conflict between spouses arises. If one spouse wins and the other loses, then eventually the entire marriage must lose. Care must be taken so that the conflict does not get out of hand and that both in the relationship achieve a degree of satisfaction — a "win-win." To most of our middle school

---

STEPS TO FACILITATE CHANGE

1. *Share a vision with both educators and community members.* Determining what your school and community want in its graduates provides a common ground for all points of view, no matter how far apart sides may appear in the beginning.

2. *Get political support in formulating change.* Be sure to involve those who assume different roles in the process.

3. *Use research.* There is a tendency to associate a proposal with the person who presents it. Research in its primary form, is neutral.

4. *Expand your thinking. Network.* Visitations and networking with different sites may offer solutions that have already been proved successful.

5. *Get ready, fire, aim.* Sometimes you just have to go ahead with a theory and work out the logistics later.

6. *Continue to monitor the change.* Make it a process that involves everyone.

7. *Reflect. Evaluate. Learn from your setbacks.* Reflection and evaluation must be incorporated after action of any type. Knowledge gathered from this process can be used as a stepping stone to bigger and better improvements.

teachers, the defeat of Pearse and Fleury's proposal was a loss.

Such was the state of mind for most of us during the rest of the winter and spring of 1993, with the result that intangible elements such as morale and job satisfaction suffered greatly. While many nonteaching members of the community may question what teacher morale and job satisfaction have to do with the day-to-day task of educating our children, author and scholar John Goodlad designates these as important pieces of a more complex characterization of school climates. In his book, *A Place Called School: Prospects for the Future,* he writes:

Schools are, first, for students. But to ignore the fact that students are influenced by teachers, who in turn are influenced by their workplace, would be to lead us once again to simplistic diagnoses and inadequate proposals for school improvement.

Satisfaction (is) a criterion of school quality. Much attention is now given in business and industry to work satisfaction, the qualities that produce it, and the relationships between workers' satisfaction and productivity.

...Relatively little attention has been given to comparable considerations in schooling. Yet the composite satisfaction of principal, teachers, students, and parents constitutes a significant indication of a school's quality, including achievement. (pp. 30-31)

Many of us were prone to consider: "If vocal factions of the community were asking us to become accountable as teachers, then we must also become responsible for our teaching conditions."

What Did We Learn from this Experience?

Lesson One:

Teachers must become educational leaders, accepting the responsibilities and accountability that go with it.

The new paradigm of teachers as formulators of policy points to a paradox in the traditional hierarchy of schooling.

Teachers' work is not structured so that (teachers) might participate in the decision making about school improvement. ...Most leadership roles currently available are not designed to change practice but to ensure the efficiency and effectiveness of the existing program. (Patricia Wasley, *Teachers Who Lead: The Rhetoric of Reform and the Realities of Practice,* pp. 3-4)

While we have always been in charge of curricular planning (beyond the traditional syllabus) in our own classrooms, it is a rather nontraditional role that needs to be addressed here. The proposal for an extra-help period for Seneca Falls Middle School children did not come to fruition, yet it is emblematic of the type of school change that must be affected by teachers who are the closest to the learning conditions of students.

I hold that this responsibility must be accepted by teachers. Will this necessarily mean a conflict in assuming new roles in implementing change in our schools? In this new scenario, the principal may no longer be the key element in school improvement. If administrative directives and decrees do not lead to the internalization of change by staff, then it is up to staff members to begin to initiate change themselves.

To support Pearse and Fleury's proposal, we had to face many community forces that did not view teachers as agents of change — those that viewed school in a custodial function, in charge of children for a set number of hours during the day while parents worked (remember the comment about the "shower schedules"); special interest groups (band/chorus in this case); and the naysayers who see teachers only as traditional employees and not as advocates of students' working conditions.

Teachers need to regard themselves as professionals and to convince other teachers to regard themselves as professionals as well. Without this credibility, the voices of those closest to the students in question will not carry much weight.

Lesson Two:
Teachers must be prepared to promote their point of view to the other decision-making groups.

School restructuring efforts have drawn attention to the sharing of power between administration, teachers, and community members. It is safe to assume that many of our middle school teachers still felt comfortable with the traditional hierarchy of decision making; to them, school boards make policy, administrators pass this on, and teachers

only involve themselves in setting the classroom conditions for learning.

Because formulating policy is still relatively new to most of us, perhaps in this instance, we didn't know how to influence the decision-making process. Ed Passifione summed up the experience this way: "I was amazed at the parent response. We really weren't prepared to sell the proposal. We weren't united."

Because of our own conviction over what we thought was a reasonable and "fair" request for the extra-help period, we entered the cafeteria that evening with the confidence that other teachers, administrators, and parents would readily support our position.

Was this a naive assumption? I raised this question over the School

Renewal Network, an IBM/NEA-sponsored computer network designed to share information electronically with specific schools, research centers, and NEA programs across the country. I received this response from Doug Fleming, NEA researcher and head of School Strategies & Options Inc., in

We could not wait for the parents, administrators, and community to accept the viewpoint of any one group of individuals, including teachers, based on "faith."

Lunenburg, Massachusetts:
Dear Mike,
Your story reminds me of something Dean Corrig-

MORE ON
READY, FIRE, AIM...

"Ready, fire, aim," is truly the essence of school improvement. Rather than analyze every step in a proposal, sometimes you just have to go ahead with a theory and work out the logistics later.

Sports broadcaster, Tim McCarver, says that in hitting a baseball, you just have to get in the batter's box and take your swings. Someone who worries about hand placement, proper grip, hip rotation, and all the little things that make up a perfect swing while the pitch is incoming will fail to accomplish anything. McCarver calls this phenomenon "paralysis through analysis."

an (dean of Texas A&M) once said in a speech: "Education is politics." That may be a bitter pill to swallow, but just because you think those persons closest to students are in the best position to influence policy, programs, and practices, doesn't mean everyone else does. Clearly, good ideas are not enough. Good ideas, by them-selves, won't get adopted. It's not enough to be a good conceptualizer; if you want your change idea to work, you must be a good politician, too. I'm using the word "politic" to mean the ability to mar-shal public opinion for or against an idea.

–Doug Fleming

Fleming's message was clear — we could not wait for the parents, administrators, and community to accept the viewpoint of any one group of individuals, including teachers, based on "faith." Top-down decrees usually encounter resistance from those not involved in the planning. In this situation, we were guilty of creating the same misgivings that we were once suspicious of ourselves.

Seneca Falls teachers needed to expand their in-fluence beyond the class-room and mobilize as a political unit to educate the community, publicize their position, and defend themselves in a positive light against negative crit-icism.

As related in Lesson 1, we had to "get our act to-gether first" before we could attempt to influence others. Faith was not enough.

Lesson Three:
When it comes to impor-tant decisions, teachers must communicate with teachers of opposing view-points to see if they can come closer to closing the ranks among faculty.

One of the three teach-ers who cast a negative vote to Pearse and Fleury's proposal was sev-enth grade social studies teacher and steering com-mittee member, Bob Klop-pel. At the parent infor-mation session, Kloppel voiced his objection to re-placing the team planning period with an additional class period on the hope that the teaming time dur-ing the morning would begin to be used for the reason we established it — to plan interdiscipli-nary curriculum and orga-nize true middle school activities. Kloppel gave me a note after the even-tual defeat of the proposal that led me to believe we weren't really that far apart philosophically and that the steering committe would soon begin to in-vestigate hopeful solu-tions to the real problems of creating a middle school.

Mike,
I'm interested in our different perceptions of this....

In my way of thinking, the real problem is not getting on the high school schedule to pick up an extra-help period, but having the flexibility we need in our schedule to accommodate LOTS of things....
Respectfully,
Bob

Lesson Four:
Administrators, teachers, and parents need to focus on a shared vision.

Another colleague of mine the other day remarked: "Who really cares what other communities do with their middle schools? We should just make ours the best we can." In the spirit of the moment, I applauded his comment.

After thinking about this a little while, I wondered if I totally agreed with him. Similar conversations have occurred in the past with comments emerging about making our middle school a viable place based on vision.

The real question here becomes, "Whose vision?" There are two sides to every coin; the failure of our proposal proves that. Teachers supporting the proposal and the parents in opposition both supported viewpoints based on their visions of what a good middle school should entail. I doubt that vindictiveness played a factor, despite some of the ferocity at the parent information session. So, for lack of consensus, which viewpoint prevails in providing direction?

Vision, as used in the context of education, has often been directly related to the experiences of those involved in the decision-making process. Much like the concept of "parenting," for example, "education" means different things to different people, with almost every viewpoint having some merit.

Involved parents tend to remember what school was like for them and attempt to incorporate the positive memories of their experiences into their decision making.

To add to this confusion, teachers as a group represent a multiplicity of opposing opinions based on individual experiences and are rarely in agreement.

In the *The Fifth Discipline: The Art and Practice of the Learning Organization*, author Peter M. Senge says that "shared vision" must be at the theoretical foundation of any organization. As applied to individuals who have the welfare of our Seneca Falls Schools at heart, shared vision may offer a focus for the energy of all the divergent factions. At its simplest, shared vision answers the question, "What do we want to create?"

From where does a shared vision emerge? I support that those involved in making decisions in our schools be allowed to access the abundant amount of research that floods our bookstores, publications, and airwaves and to view the data available from professional organizations and national resource centers. Representatives on opposing sides of the issues may scoff that they don't have time for professional educational reading. My question is, "What distinguishes teaching from other professions?" I would personally be concerned for my family if our local doctor and dentist didn't have time to keep up on the latest surgical techniques or information on safety procedures or new medications.

Can we choose to ignore the findings of Howard Gardner on human intelligence, or those of Theodore Sizer on efficient reorganization of schools, or the Breadloaf Project in student-centered reading and writing in creating our vision of school? Think about the truth of the statement, "We teach as we have been taught." To me, this translates into, "Our school as we have been schooled." Somehow this is a statement that we, as concerned adults who are to be entrusted with the education of the next generation's children, must seriously address.

Once conflicting sides begin to view current research (even though it may be a "task" in the beginning), then steps will be taken to ensure a shared vision for kids in Seneca Falls (with the result that there may someday no longer be "sides"). After all, do we tolerate a child in our classroom who declines to accept the search for truth? Then, why do we tolerate this behavior from those adults deciding his or her educational future? Educating the community and directing the focus on student outcomes becomes an important lesson.

Lesson Five:
Piecemeal change won't do.

There is a "ripple effect" that exists in schools; what happens in one area, affects another.

Acceptance of the schedule change proposal would have provided extra instructional time for middle school students, but possibly eliminated the morning band/chorus program and minimized the input of the special area teachers in our team decision-making, even though most of these teachers were willing to give up this participation to support the extra-help proposal. The schedule change would have been a piecemeal change that did not really solve the larger problem of creating a system that will effectively prepare our students for graduation. Since we became a middle school, we have been attempting to create a culture separate from the high school, but have been unsuccessful because of the economic necessity for crossover

staff to teach in both buildings. Efforts by teacher groups and our respective building and district steering committees to develop a solution effectively dividing the buildings have been in vain.

Because simple solutions create ripples in others' areas, tinkering is out; a total restructuring of the system must emerge, producing a "win-win" situation for the staff of both buildings, the students, and the community.

Lesson Six:
Parents representing all interests need to get involved in school decisions.

It appeared to me that many of the parents who attended the parent information night represented the band and chorus interests since these programs were perceived to be in immediate danger from the proposed change in schedule. While I am happy to see this large turnout under normal circumstances, this time I was somewhat dubious about the lack of representation of other parental concerns in the community. The basis for the proposal was to provide additional instructional time for students in need. Traditionally, parents of students deemed "in need" do not often find their way to school meetings. The conclusions of Arthur Powell, Eleanor Farrar, and David Cohen in *The Shopping Mall High School: Winners and Losers in the Educational Marketplace* equate the special interest groups of school parents to be as powerful in determining school policy as political lobbyists are in influencing Congressional directives.

Amidst the hoopla of protecting the band/chorus program and preserving the morning teaching time, there remained no satisfactory resolution to the problem of providing extra-help time to middle school students who need it. We must remember that the school teaches *all* children. If *all* parents were in attendance, the proposal at least would have had a truly representative hearing.

Lesson Seven:
There must be commitment to the truth.

Schools, like businesses, need to search inside to see if they are delivering what is promised. This role of education (school, if you like) may not necessarily reflect the views of the community, but may lead in the shaping of the community's views. To this, Senge adds:

"Shared vision can generate levels of creative tensions that go far beyond individuals' comfort levels. Those who contribute the most toward realizing a lofty vision will be those who can hold this creative tension: remain clear on the vision and continue to inquire into current reality." (1990)

Even after the defeat of the proposal last winter, most faculty members are seeking ways to serve the needs of students in need of extra help. They are asking: What are some other ways that we can give extra individualized help to our middle school students? Do our achievement scores denote a problem in specific areas that might indicate that additional time is necessary? Should Pearse and Fleury resubmit their proposal? Are there implications here that may address the ratio of teachers to parents on the steering committee?

Even though politics are present in education, is this inherently bad if the focus is on improving educational quality?

Seneca Falls Today

Time and experience have softened the hard edges of last winter's positions.

School restructuring is the art of transforming adversity into opportunity.

The months in passing have allowed us to reflect on our roles as policymakers in the middle school. We are now more understanding of the implementation processes and a little more aware of the interconnectedness of all aspects of our school climate.

As a classroom teacher, Bob Kloppel knows the value of the extra-help period. His project-oriented

Change gets into people's comfort zones.

course requires students to go beyond the 40 minutes they spend daily in his classroom. Kloppel reflects: "To my way of thinking, they wanted to go backward, to re-establish something that would have seriously injured the middle school. Although I oppose the idea of the extra-help period, I do recognize, of course, that the concept of extra help is

important in middle school. I expect that we will be tackling this issue again, maybe sooner than we think."

Lee Foster, 1993-94 steering committee faculty chair seconds Kloppel's hopes. "We now have more facts and figures than we had before. As a group, we must support the idea of extra help that influences the high expectations we have for our students and may result in better test scores — not as a change in existing programs. I have the feeling that if a proposal was thoughtfully put together and submitted to the steering committee this year, it might have a better shot."

Summary

I admit that in some places, this story has bordered on the melodramatic. I have attempted herein to tell the tale of a middle school staff who demonstrated a deep caring for the children of our community by reorganizing its contact time for students in need. Not only was its proposal defeated, but those who took the risk of advancing the idea were subjected to an experience that left them feeling powerless. Some teachers still harbor twinges of bitterness today. However, I feel that, as a group, we have risen from the ashes of our defeat, perhaps a little warier, definitely a little wiser. I truly believe the statement of the philosopher, Nietzche, "What doesn't' kill you makes you stronger." Carl Luty, an editor of *Doubts and Certainties* newsletter, took this to a newer context when he wrote in the September 1992 edition: "School restructuring is the art of transforming adversity into opportunity."

We have made the attempts to transform adversity into opportunity in the Seneca Falls Middle School, and I sense that our input is beginning to net results. In the summer of 1992, I spent four long days doing work for our School Improvement Team, which could best be described as "frustrating." In comparison, in the summer of '93, I felt our efforts progressed smoothly and more efficiently. In other recent summer work, middle school expert Marla Steele conducted an inservice workshop for the entire faculty to help us establish our vision of a successful middle school. Seven of us worked on the organization of our advisor/advisee program and other teachers serving on committees for portfolio and performance assessment did summer work as well. For the first time as a "middle school department," Ron Fleury, Don Lohr (seventh grade math), and Candy Pirwitz (sixth grade math) met to evaluate a new comprehensive mathematics program. This year, faculty meetings will occur on a weekly basis to facilitate closer communication with all teachers. It appears that ownership of the middle school climate is being fairly distributed.

Whether lasting decisions are made or not, people are involved in the process. Michael Fullan of the Faculty of Education at the University of Toronto, says, "Change is a journey, not a blueprint. ...What is needed is a guided journey."

I cannot predict what the future will hold for the Seneca Falls School District. Since the proposal to add extra-help time was defeated, community members and teaching staff have been buzzing more than ever about the middle school. Discussion about alternative scheduling, a look into integrated curriculum and other educational innovations are starting to wind their way into our professional conversations. "Vision" has become a key word. Next to Goulds Pumps and athletic excellence, the teaching staff, students, and parents in Seneca Falls may soon be boasting about their middle school as well. ◆

On Not Giving Up

By Doug Fleming

There have been a lot of "success" stories concerning school renewal efforts — instances where events went as planned, where significant changes were introduced and accepted in schools and districts. There have also been some painful stories — episodes where, despite a consensus among staff, the support needed to sustain a change was withheld by administrators, parents, the school board, or community members. It's hard to bounce back from a defeat like that, to dust yourself off and get back in the game when your best intentions may have been misinterpreted, misunderstood, or even publicly devalued. It's even harder to give advice to anyone who still feels the sting of that defeat.

But the following story is tangible testimony to the importance of not giving up.

In 1985, Microbits Peripheral Products, Inc., of Albany, Oregon, went belly up. John Wiley and Alan Ackerman lost everything when the Atari computer market collapsed. They had put all their eggs in one basket, and the basket disappeared. They could have quit right there, stopped doing everything from assembly to shipping, got sensible jobs, and had a life — but they believed in themselves and their product.

Wiley and Ackerman found 10 local investors who helped put them back in business. They concentrated on what each of them could do best, instead of trying to do everything themselves. They hired others to handle tasks that did not draw on their strengths. They instituted financial planning and reporting procedures. Most importantly, they committed themselves to developing new products for different brands of computers, so their business would not be too dependent on the fortunes of any one company.

You may not recognize the names Wiley and Ackerman, but you may very well own one of their Supra computer modems. You might like to know that last year Supra Corporation had 100 employees, a new 25,000-square-foot building, and $35 million in sales, largely because these two guys wouldn't roll over and play dead.

Wiley admits, "I'm not proud that I ran a company that failed; I'm proud that I now run one that is successful. Failure always slows you down. But if you have determination and a desire to learn, it won't stop you."

Author: Doug Fleming is co-founder of School Strategies & Options, Inc., in Lunenburg, Massachusetts.
Source: This essay first appeared on the IBM/NEA-sponsored School Renewal Network.

Reader Reflections

Insights: _____

_____

_____

_____

_____

Actions for Our School (District) to Consider: _____

_____

_____

_____

_____

_____

_____

_____

Appendix

RESTRUCTURING SCHOOLS:
A Systemic View

FROM:
A Traditional School System

A Continuum of Change

TO:
A Learning Community

Structure and Organization

- Teacher isolation
- Centralized decision making
- Parents, business, and others as visitors
- External "expert" staff development programs
- Teacher role viewed as time with students

Structure and Organization

- Teacher collaboration
- Site-based decision making inclusive of faculty and staff
- Parents, business, and others as partners and decision makers
- Internal shared professional development
- Teacher role expanded to include planning, decision making, and other professional duties

Source: Robert McClure, *A Resource Guide for School Improvement*, NEA Professional Library, Forthcoming.

RESTRUCTURING SCHOOLS:
A Systemic View

A Continuum of Change

FROM:
A Traditional School System

TO:
A Learning Community

Teaching and Learning

- Teacher as worker; student as product

- Students in passive (instructional) settings

- Isolated competitive setting for students and teachers

- "Four walls" and 40 minutes as classroom

- Homogeneous grouping

Teaching and Learning

- Teacher as leader/facilitator; student as worker

- Students in active, constructional settings

- Cooperative, collegial settings for students and teachers

- Learning environment flexible as to time and place

- Flexible, heterogeneous groups

Source: Robert McClure, *A Resource Guide for School Improvement,* NEA Professional Library, Forthcoming.

RESTRUCTURING SCHOOLS:
A Systemic View

FROM:
A Traditional School System

A Continuum of Change

TO:
A Learning Community

Curriculum

- Learning in a "school only" context

- Focus on covering content

- Fragmented separate subjects

- Emphasis on "knowing"

- Standardized content for all

Curriculum

- Learning in a life context

- Focus on understanding concepts

- Integrated holistic learning

- Emphasis on "learning"

- Individualized programs

Source: Robert McClure, *A Resource Guide for School Improvement,* NEA Professional Library, Forthcoming.

RESTRUCTURING SCHOOLS:
A Systemic View

FROM:
A Traditional School System

→ **A Continuum of Change** →

TO:
A Learning Community

Assessment and Accountability

- Priority placed on standardized testing

- Evaluative reporting systems, emphasizing "can't do"

- Judgments based on bell curve

- Faculty assessment as once a year, top down

- School accountability based on standardized test scores

Assessment and Accountability

- Multiple, authentic assessment options for students

- Descriptive reporting systems that emphasize "can do"

- Every child can and will learn

- Faculty assessment as continual, collegial, professional development

- Accountability measured by meeting output standards

Source: Robert McClure, *A Resource Guide for School Improvement*, NEA Professional Library, Forthcoming.

Selected Resources

Books

Alverman, G., et al. 1991. *National Reading Research Center: A Proposal*. Athens, Ga., and College Park, Md.: University of Georgia and University of Maryland.

Bailey, W. J. 1991. *School Site-Management Applied*. Lancaster, Penn.: Technomic.

Barrett, P., ed. 1991. *Doubts and Certainties: Working Together to Restructure Schools*. Washington, D.C.: National Education Association.

The Best of Success: A Handbook of Success Ideas. 1984. Lombard, Ill.: Great Quotations.

Clune, W., and White, P. 1988. *School-Based Management: Institutional Variation, Implementation, and Issues for Further Research*. New Brunswick, N.J.: Center for Policy Research in Education.

Cochran-Smith, M., Lytle, S. L., editors. 1992. *Inside/Outside: Teacher Research and Knowledge*. New York: Teachers College Press.

Elmore, R. F. 1990. *Restructuring Schools: The Next Generation of Educational Reform*. San Francisco: Jossey-Bass.

Erb, T. O., and Doda, N. M. 1989. *Team Organization: Promise, Practices, and Possibilities*. Washington, D.C.: National Education Association.

Etheridge, C. P., Horgan, D., Valesky, T., Hall, M., and Terrell, L. 1994. *Challenge to Change: The Memphis Experience with School-Based Decision Making*. Washington, D.C.: National Education Association.

Gibbs, J. R. 1978. *Trust: A New View of Personal and Organizational Change*. Cardiff, Calif.: Omicron Press.

Fiske, E. 1992. *Smart Schools, Smart Kids: Why Do Some Schools Work?* New York: Touchstone.

Fullan, M. 1982. *The Meaning of Educational Change*. Toronto, Ontario, Canada: Ontario Institute for Studies in Education Press.

Fullan, M., and Stiegelbauer, S. 1991. *The New Meaning of Educational Change*. New York: Teachers College Press.

Glatthorn, A. A. 1992. *Teachers as Agents of Change: A New Look at School Improvement*. Washington, D.C.: National Education Association.

Good, T. L., and Brophy, J. E. 1991. *Looking into Classrooms*. New York: Harper and Row.

Goodlad, J. I. 1984. *A Place Called School: Prospects for the Future.* New York: McGraw-Hill.

Hess, G. A. 1991. *School Restructuring, Chicago Style.* Newbury, Calif.: Corwin Press.

Larson, L. L. 1992. *Changing Schools from the Inside Out.* Lancaster, Penn.: Technomic.

Lieberman, A., ed. 1986. *Teachers Who Lead.* New York: Teachers College Press.

Livingston, C, ed. 1991. *Teachers as Leaders.* Washington, D.C.: National Education Association.

Livingston, C., and Castle, S. 1993. *Teachers and Research in Action.* Washington, D.C.: National Education Association.

Maeroff, G. I. 1988. *The Empowerment of Teachers.* New York: Teachers College Press.

Maeroff, G. I. 1993. *Team Building for School Change.* New York: Teachers College Press.

Martz, L. 1992. *Making Schools Better: How Parents and Teachers Across the Country Are Taking Action— And How You Can , Too.* New York: Time Books.

Murphy, J. 1991. *Restructuring Schools: Capturing and Assessing the Phenomena.* New York: Teachers College Press.

Powell, A., Farrar, E., and Cohen, D. 1985. *The Shopping Mall High School: Winners and Losers in the Educational Marketplace.* Boston: Houghton Mifflin.

Sarason, S. 1990. *The Predictable Failure of Educational Reform.* San Francisco: Jossey-Bass.

Senge, P. 1990. *The Fifth Discipline: The Art and Practice of the Learning Organization.* New York: Doubleday.

Sizer, T. R. 1992. *Horace's School: Redesigning the American High School.* Boston: Houghton Mifflin.

Wasley, P. 1991. *Teachers Who Lead: The Rhetoric of Reform and the Realities of Practice.* New York: Teachers College Press.

Articles, Papers, and Reports

Cole, R., and Schlechty, P. 1992. "Teachers as Trailblazers." *Educational Horizons,* Spring, 135-37.

Cushman, K. 1992. "What Works, What Doesn't: Lessons from Essential School Reform." *The Coalition of Essential Schools,* 9(11): 1-8.

Fullan, M. G. 1992. "Visions that Blind." *Educational Leadership,* 49(5):19-20.

Gusky, T. 1990. "Integrating Innovations." *Educational Leadership,* 47(5): 11-15.

Joyce, B. 1991. "The Doors to School Improvement." *Educational Leadership,* 48(8): 59-62.

Kelley, D., and Conner, D. R. 1979. "The Emotional Cycle of Change." In *The 1979 Annual Handbook for Group Facilitators.* La Jolla, Calif.: University Associates.

Monson, M. P., and Monson, R. J. 1993. "Who Creates Curriculum? New Roles for Teachers." *Educational Leadership,* 51(2) 19-21.

O'Flahavan, J. F. 1991. "Emphasizing the Teacher in Teacher Research Communities," *Reading Teacher,* 9(1).

O'Flahavan, J. F. 1993. "Teacher Research in an Era of School Reform," *Greater Washington Reading Council Journal,* 17, 32-34.

O'Flahavan, J. F. 1993. "Teacher Researchers, Administrators, Students Teachers, Students, and University Professors at Work: Charting the Evolution of a School Research Center." University of Maryland: National Reading Research Center. Year II, continuation of project proposal.

O'Neil, J. 1993. "Turning the System on Its Head." *Educational Leadership,* 51(1): 8-13.

Spady, W. G. 1988. "Organizing for Results: The Basis for Authentic Restructuring and Reform." *Educational Leadership,* 46(2): 4-8.

Weissglass, J. 1991. "Teachers Have Feelings: What Can We Do About It?" *Journal of Staff Development,* 12 (1): 28-33.

Newsletters and Journals

Doubts and Certainties. A newsletter on school transformation, published by the National Education Association's National Center for Innovation. 1201 16th St., NW, Washington, D.C. 20036.

Teaching and Change. A journal in which teachers share their studies and stories about implementing changes in classroom practice. A joint publication of the NEA Professional Library and Corwin Press, Inc. Thousand Oaks, Calif.: A Sage Publications Company.

Video

1993. *Outcomes-Based Education—Learning for a Better Future.* National Cassette Services, Inc. P.O. Box 99, Front Royal, VA 22630.

Organizations

The High Success Network, P.O. Box 1630, Eagle, CO 81631.

School Strategies and Options, P.O. Box 1705, Lunenberg, MA 01462.

Notes:

_____

_____

_____

_____

_____

_____

Glossary

Climate
The shared perceptions of the way things are. In other words, the shared perceptions that those associated with a school have about its policies, practices, and procedures.

Collegiality
Collaborative teamwork that marshals the best efforts of all concerned.

Collegial Leadership
Situations in which leadership is distributed among colleagues (i.e., among instructional teams).

Culture
The system of shared meanings, assumptions, and underlying values (or philosophy) of an organization.

Exit Outcome
Specific competency a school wants its students to accomplish by the time they graduate.

Mission
The central purpose of the school. The mission of a school is usually articulated in a *mission statement*.

Norms
The standard of behavior to which people conform. The climate and culture of a school produce the norms.

Outcome
Learning behavior or competency.

Paradigm
An accepted model or pattern that gains its initial status because it is seemingly more successful than competitors in solving acute problems.

School-Based Management
A system of administration in which the school is the primary unit of educational decision making. (Sometimes called site-based management. Involves collegial leadership.)

Vision
One's dream of what one's school should be. The school's mission is often reflected in this vision.

"All people ever have is their own understanding.
You can tell them all sorts of things,
but you can't make them believe anything unless
they also construct the information for themselves."

Eleanor Duckworth
Harvard University